FROM AND CO... THE CROSS OF CHRIST

The Testimony of a Former Hindu

PREMA SANKARSINGH PELLETIER

Author contact information:
Prema Pelletier
P.O. Box 875
Moravian Falls, North Carolina 28654-0875
USA
Email: PremaPelletier77@gmail.com

Cover design and layout:
Michael McDonald
Email: artfx2@gmail.com

Individuals and church groups may order books directly from the publisher. Retailers and wholesalers should order from our distributors. Refer to the Deeper Revelation Books website for distribution information, as well as an online catalog of all our books.

Published by:

Deeper Revelation Books
Revealing "the deep things of God" (1 Cor. 2:10)
P.O. Box 4260
Cleveland, TN 37320 423-478-2843
Website: *www.deeperrevelationbooks.org*
Email: *info@deeperrevelationbooks.org*

Deeper Revelation Books assists Christian authors in publishing and distributing their books. Final responsibility for design, content, permissions, editorial accuracy, and doctrinal views, either expressed or implied, belongs to the author.

DEDICATION

To my gracious and loving heavenly Father, my lovely Lord and Savior Jesus Christ, and my wonderful, comforting Counselor, the Holy Spirit, be all the glory, honor, praise, and credit for the miraculous, redemptive story revealed through these pages.

Thank You, my Lord and my God, for rescuing me from darkness and using my life to touch others with Your light. All glory, praise, honor, and credit belong to You. I lay my life at Your feet and declare that there is no God like You!

The true story of a lonely, suicidal, hopeless, and rejected Hindu woman whose life was completely changed when she encountered Jesus Christ.

ACKNOWLEDGMENTS

I shared my testimony with Pastor Mike Shreve one evening after he ministered at Living Water Christian Fellowship in North Wilkesboro, North Carolina. He immediately encouraged me to write a book. Unknown to him, I had already completed a manuscript years before but had not done anything with it. This is an updated version. Thank you, Pastor Mike Shreve, and every one of your fine staff at Deeper Revelation Books, for helping me to bring this book to fruition. Being a new writer and not knowing what to expect, I quickly found that I had nothing to worry about. My telephone calls and questions were always answered promptly, with patience and with such courtesy. Fine editing, great artwork. Excellent service!

I would also like to thank each and every one who has been such a help and blessing in my life, and who has faithfully stood with me. May the Lord bless all of you for being so gracious.

CONTENTS

Chapter 1
How It All Started

Leaving Calcutta (Kolkata) behind, my Hindu ancestors left India in 1845 and sailed to the island of Trinidad in the West Indies. They came as indentured servants to work on the sugar plantations for the British.

My great-grandmother was only seven years old when she arrived with her parents. They knew no English and spoke only Hindi and Bengali. My great-grandfather was from Uttar Pradesh in Northern India. He left there as a young man, and though he knew no English, he worked hard and became a well-to-do landowner and moneylender. He died when I was a young child, and after that my family changed their last name from Shankar to Sankar. However, though the name was changed, my ancestors never deviated from their strong Hindu religion, culture, customs, language, food, and dress. These things they fiercely protected.

My ancestors were contracted out for five to ten years upon their arrival, and then they were given the choice to remain in Trinidad or return to India. They chose to stay and make a new life for themselves and their children. Although my great-grandmother never learned English, her three children learned the local dialect as well as Hindi and Bengali. When there were confidential matters to be discussed, they communicated in Hindi, much to the amusement (and sometimes frustration!) of the younger generations. We knew how to sing any song in Hindi but never learned to speak the language fluently.

The main language that is spoken in Trinidad is an English Creole dialect. English is the country's official language, but to learn how to speak and write it properly, one has to go to school.

My father was a first-generation Indian Trinidadian. His father had migrated from the state of Punjab with his parents when he was just a boy and spoke only Punjabi. My dad was proud of being a Sikh of the Khatri caste. However, the family worshiped the Hindu way.

Growing up in Trinidad allowed me to have a fairly good understanding of both cultures, the East and the West. However, I was born on the grounds of a Hindu temple and was raised as a Hindu. We never accepted the Name of Jesus and knew nothing about the Bible. To my family, Jesus was just another word and had no significant meaning to them.

My Ma and Pa

The Sankars lived on Sankar Street (a street named after my great-grandfather) in a small town called Tunapuna, about eight miles from the capital city of Port of Spain. I was raised by my maternal grandmother whom I called Ma. She loved me as dearly as she loved her own children. I also adored my Ma and loved the rest of my family.

My strict grandfather, whom I addressed as Pa, would often be found standing for hours with one leg propped against the other, praying and worshiping in our temple. His usual chant was the Hindu sacred sound that every Hindu repeats, the word "Aum," also pronounced as "Om." It is symbolized as ॐ and represents the ultimate sound of the universe. This chant is said to represent God in three ways: A for Brahma, U for Vishnu, and M for Shiva. This chant is often used by those practicing yoga.

As in most Indian homes, Pa didn't take much part in raising the children. That was Ma's responsibility. However, he did enforce the rules. One such rule was never to look at a person in the eyes when speaking with them. In our culture, looking at someone in the eyes meant you were disrespecting him or her and being rude. So, we were taught to keep our heads down, just glance, never look directly at someone, and never to stare.

It took me years to overcome this rule after I was told by someone in Canada that one way to show respect to someone is to actually look at them. At that time, I was a Christian and had read in the Bible that the eyes are the window – or the mirror – of the soul and that the light of the body is the eye. Therefore, a person's true motives and thoughts can be more easily discerned by looking into his or her eyes.

Another rule was to always show respect to older people. Always address them as auntie, uncle, neighbor, Mr. or Mrs., whether you knew them or not. Also, always say "thank you" and "please." We children were never allowed to sit among the elders. Just one telling look sent us scattering for cover.

My Ma was a very good, very kind, very pious, and very respectable lady. I also had wonderful aunts and uncles. My family was not perfect, but nonetheless, they were good, decent, hard-working, first-and-second-generation Indian Trinidadians who believed in working diligently and responsibly to establish their lives. It was through their hard work that they achieved what they had while also helping many others.

Ma, who was so full of love, was the primary person who took care of the many people working for us in our commercial farming business. Most Hindu fathers preferred to send their sons to school but not their daughters. According to the Hindu traditions at that time, Ma didn't have a single day of schooling. Yet, she was a very wise lady who handled the business aspects with much care and common sense. It was a joke among us that Ma never attended school, but she sure knew how to count the dollars.

At the end of the season, most of the crops were sold to the Marketing Board which, in turn, exported the produce to America and Canada. Rice, sugarcane, cucumbers, pumpkins, ochroes (okras), eggplants, tomatoes, ginger, and other vegetables were harvested by the truckloads.

Ma always made sure that the workers were paid on time. She was never stingy with what she had but was a very generous lady who even shared meals with the workers. She was full of compassion and love, and I admired her so much. She was a gentle soul, a loving, sweet, and wise lady who raised me with her heart. I love her so! To me, she was the most perfect lady on the earth. Although it has been many years since she passed away, I still feel this way about my precious Ma.

Lacking Nothing, but Empty in My Soul

In spite of lacking nothing, there was this cry, this haunting emptiness, in my soul which I didn't understand. "Maybe it is just me," I would think. It would take many great heartaches and deep emotional pains to help me realize that there is more to life than just living and going through the motions. One day, I was jolted from believing in the many birth cycles of reincarnation, which is an easily accepted part of the Hindu belief system, to the understanding that, *"It is appointed unto men once to die, but after this the judgment."* (Hebrews 9:27)

It took so much more than living the way I was raised to find this hope, truth, and peace. It took the Creator, my heavenly Father, to open my blind spiritual eyes and reveal His divine, unconditional love to me through His Son, Jesus Christ, and through His Holy Spirit.

In short, God gave me a life-changing miracle – from worshiping cows to worshiping the Creator of the cow; from worshiping the image of the cobra snake, and being a part of live cobra worship in India, to opening my spiritual eyes to His love and light. What a lost and blind soul I was. Such was the magnitude of my spiritual ignorance and blindness.

Indeed, I understand why my beloved Hindu brothers, sisters, mothers, and fathers worship the way they do. God Himself has to reveal truth to their precious hearts and to everyone else's heart.

The Bible promises that if we will search for God with all our hearts, He will be found of us. The living and true God has good plans for His creation, but first we must know Him through His Son, Jesus Christ, Who is Lord of all.

The Bible also says in 2 Corinthians 4:3–4:

But if our Gospel be hid, it is hid to them that are lost:

In whom the god of this world [meaning the devil] *hath blinded the minds of them which believe not, lest the light of the glorious Gospel of Christ, Who is the image of God, should shine unto them.*

I cannot thank my Lord Jesus enough for revealing the truth of His Gospel to my soul, which every human being needs.

You might be thinking, "But how did all this start? What made you turn away from your Hindu religion that was such an important part of your life?" While most Hindus would have a simple shrine with one or two deities in their house, we were the proud Indians with a Hindu temple in our yard. It was not a large temple, but nonetheless, it was a landmark on our property and was there from as far back as I can remember. We were sometimes referred to as "the people with the temple on Sankar Street."

15

During my journey, I have come to understand that being religious or having an abundance of material things are both insufficient to satisfy the soul. We must be connected to the Creator of our soul, the living and true God, Jesus Christ, or else life is just a blur, an aimless existence under a well-hidden pretense. I have been there. I was a walking dead frame of a human being, smiling through my pain, but doomed for the place where all unbelievers go, that terrible place that Jesus warned us about called hell. How I thank my Father in heaven for making a way of escape for all true believers through the death, burial, and resurrection of His Son, Jesus Christ!

The Bible says in John 1:10–12:

He was in the world, and the world was made by Him, and the world knew Him not.

He came unto His own, and His own received Him not.

But as many as received Him, to them gave He power to become the sons of God, even to them that believe on His Name.

The saddest part of it all is that I was so unaware of where I was headed. I knew something was missing but didn't know what to do about it. Eventually I found out, but only after much pain and sorrow.

Now, I must share a little about the religious background into which I was born and in which I was raised. For some of you reading this book, it will be an astonishing eyeopener.

CHAPTER 2
WHAT HINDUS BELIEVE

To my beloved Hindu brothers and sisters, and everyone else who reads this book, my heart's desire is to see you in heaven.

My questions to you are, "Who do you think God is? What is your understanding of Him? And what is the nature of your relationship with Him?"

There is a difference between truth and understanding. Truth is reality as it actually is. Understanding is our own, personal, mental grasp of that reality. Truth is always fully accurate and correct. Our understanding of truth, however, may be correct, partially correct, or totally false.

A roadmap is comparable to understanding. If it is an accurate representation of the land it portrays, then it can be most helpful indeed. However, if it contains errors, it can lead us in the wrong direction, and we can get lost.

The issue is never what the understanding of others is. The issue is always what the truth is. The understanding of others may be correct, partially correct, or totally false. Even many people having the same understanding of something does not make that view correct. Mass deception is an unfortunate aspect of the human condition and of history.

Nor is the issue whether or not we are sincere in our beliefs. We can be totally sincere and totally wrong at the same time.

Passionate sincerity for a false belief system can ultimately have disastrous results.

For example, I was born into a Hindu family and was raised as a Hindu. My understanding was that all the views of everyone around me were correct. I assumed, as just about all young children do, that whatever I was taught was true. Surely, my parents, teachers, religious leaders, and all the other people around me in my culture who were older and wiser than I, surely, they must all be right.

There is a very common expression which many of us have used at one time or another. We refer to someone as being "born a Hindu."

The reality is more accurately expressed by saying that I was born into a Hindu family and was raised in the Hindu teachings. As I grew up, I assumed that everything I was taught was true.

Unlike Christians who worship one God, Hindus worship over three hundred and thirty million gods (the traditional number). Some say thirty-three million. In Hinduism, everything is connected with life and life cycles: past, present, and future. A major tenet of Hinduism is the belief of reincarnation, which is a continuous cycle of life. It takes place when a departed soul, which is seen as eternal and part of the spiritual realm, returns to the physical realm in a new body. During this cycle of being reincarnated, one can take the form of anything, including a dog, cat, goat, fly, bird, snake, or another human being, depending on what kind of deeds that the person being "recycled" has achieved.

A soul will complete this cycle several thousand times, some say about eighty-four thousand, reincarnating into different forms each time, learning new things and working through its karma. Karma is the result of good and bad deeds, a type of cause and effect. Hindus believe that part of their higher enlightenment is found right inside them, giving one the status of being a god.

Among the millions of gods and goddesses worshiped, Brahma is considered the creator, Vishnu the preserver, and Shiva is worshiped as the destroyer or transformer. These three deities have been called the "Trimurti," the "Hindu triad," or the "great trinity." Shiva wears a cobra snake, Vasuki Naagraj, the King of Snakes, draped around his neck.

There are also considered to be three major goddesses, Saraswati, Lakshmi, and Parvati, which together are sometimes called the "Tridevi," being either a feminine version of the Trimurti or their consorts. Devi is the Sanskrit word for goddess, the masculine form being Deva.

In Hinduism, the major gods and goddesses can manifest in various forms, thereby appearing as innumerable other deities, each with its own name. Therefore, one deity can also be known by many other names, each of which is considered to be one of its forms. Among the various Hindu groups, there is no total agreement as to the lineup and relative importance of the various gods and goddesses.

Thus Parvati, the wife of Shiva, is considered an incarnation of Adi Parashakti, sometimes simply called Shakti, and Durga is considered a manifestation of Parvati. These deities are considered to be the greatest goddess, the mother of the universe.

Durga is a popular goddess of war, frequently depicted standing atop or riding a tiger or a lion. Her name means "invincible." She is multi-limbed, having between eight and eighteen hands, each of which holds a weapon. Regarded as a warrior who combats evils and demonic forces, her weapons are considered to be symbolical of virtues.

Kali has been related to Adi Parashakti, Parvati, and Durga and thereby is associated with Shiva. She is a fierce warrior in the extreme, with her hair disheveled, corpses of children as her earrings, a garland of skulls about her neck, and a skirt of human arms about her waist. In some artwork, she has been depicted with one of her four arms bearing a sabre, another a severed head, and yet another a bowl collecting the blood of the severed head. Yet, she is still considered to be a good goddess, and her attributes have been interpreted to be positive.

Both Durga and Kali are worshiped by blood sacrifice.

The sun is also worshiped as a god, and it was not an unusual thing to see my great-grandmother stand and stare at the sun for hours every morning while she worshiped.

Agni is the fire god, taking the form of fire on the earth, lightning in the atmosphere, and the fire of the sun in the heavens. As many sacrifices are made with fire, he is considered to be the carrier of such offerings to the gods.

Major traditional rites-of-passage rituals involve fire, and so Agni is considered to play a major role in them. He is regarded as the central witness in a Hindu marriage to the seven wedding vows of the bride and groom, each one made as they walk around the sacred fire. It is also a form of Agni that cremates the body on the funeral pyre at the end of a Hindu's earthly life.

Gods in Animal Form

Hindus' respect for a mother raises the status of a cow to a goddess. It is regarded as a sacred symbol of life as it gives life-sustaining milk. According to the oldest Hindu scriptures, the Vedas, the cow is associated with the mother of all the gods, Aditi. The majority of Hindus are vegetarians, but even most non-vegetarian Hindus will not eat beef.

Hindus worship snakes as gods. The cobra is considered the most sacred snake in India. I mentioned that Shiva is presented as having one wrapped around his neck. Nag Panchami is an important festival which is devoted to the worship of snakes.

Throughout India, there are countless snake temples. These contain both images of cobras and living snakes, which are offered prayers, milk, and incense. Newlyweds and childless couples go to some of these temples for the purpose of offering prayers to have children. In Hinduism, a childless woman is considered cursed.

The Naga Puja is a religious ritual which is performed mainly to appease nagas (serpent spirits) which have been offended, or to please them. It is considered a sin to kill a snake as one is killing one of his gods. If one is killed accidentally, a naga puja has to be performed.

Ganesha is one of the most worshiped and easily recognized of the Hindu gods, having the head of an elephant, and a human body with a large belly. Regarded as the god of new beginnings, success, wisdom, and the remover of obstacles, he is often worshiped at the beginning of anything new.

Another popular and easily recognized god is Hanuman, the monkey god. He is regarded as the spiritual son of Vayu, the wind god. The various gods of Hinduism are presented as having specific virtues, and he is no exception. The Hanuman Chalisa is a forty-verse devotional hymn addressed to him which details his various qualities. It is one of the bestselling Hindu religious books and is said to be recited by millions of Hindus every day.

The Temple of Rats located in Deshnoke, Rajastan, also known as the Karni Mata Temple, houses approximately twenty-five thousand black rats which are considered holy. The few white ones found among them are thought to be more holy. It is said that Laxman, the son of Karni Mata, drowned in a pond and was brought back to life by Yama, the god of death. The agreement was that Laxman and all of Karni Mata's male children would be reincarnated as rats.

A list of what Hindus consider to be gods, and what they worship, would be endless. Things which they consider to be sacred include the moon, the sea, rivers, ponds, trees, rocks, statues, icons, and many other objects.

In our temple and in our house, many deities (including cows, cobras, monkeys, and elephants) were displayed as statues, or as pictures which hung on the walls. These were just a tiny fraction of the gods we worshiped.

In certain castes and sects of Hinduism, blood sacrifices of animals or birds are very much a part of their worship. In our own religious activities, animals were never sacrificed, but milk, fruit, flowers, and incense were always part of the ritual.

The bottom line is that Hindus believe man is divine and achieves his own level of spirituality as he continues on this very tedious journey of penance and good works. In Hinduism, just about everything and everyone is a god.

Hinduism was not founded by any one person. Rather, it is a compilation of many traditions and philosophies, with its origins dating back at least 3,500 years and beyond, beginning most likely in the Indus Valley. Many Hindus maintain that their religion is timeless and has always existed.

Diwali

When celebrating the festivals, my Ma paid special attention to the most important one, Diwali, also known as the Festival of Lights. This holiday is celebrated to honor Ramachandra, who is believed to be the incarnation of the god Vishnu. On this day, light is celebrated as being dominant over darkness and good over evil. It is also believed that Rama returned from Ayodhya after fourteen years of exile, where he had fought and won a battle against demons and the demon king, Ravana. The worship of Lakshmi, the goddess of wealth, is also a very dominant Diwali tradition.

In our home, as we celebrated the festival of Diwali, every family member took part in lighting thousands of diyas, which are small clay pots housed with cotton wicks and oil. This process would begin sharply at six in the evening, and when lit, these diyas were displayed with great pride all over the house and large yard.

My Ma finished the ceremony with special prayers that she learned to perform from her parents and from seeing the movements of the pundit (a Hindu priest). Afterward, she would place a tika or bindi, which is a colorful dot, on our foreheads between the eyebrows. This area is supposed to be the "third eye chakra," chakras being spiritual energy centers within the human body. A widow will wear a black tika to show her grief.

Then it was time for celebration. Bhajans (religious songs) played loudly from our brightly lit temple. There was food in abundance, wonderful Indian desserts, rejoicing, and much festivity.

Firecrackers were also plentiful on Diwali night to ward off evil spirits. As the evening wore on, we all made the rounds with more oil, wicks, and matches to keep the diyas brightly lit until it was time to retire for the night. For us children, it was a happy time as we celebrated this important festival.

In sharing about my upbringing, people sometimes ask if I really believed these things. My answer is simple: blind people cannot see, even in the light, and that goes for either spiritual or physical blindness.

I was once a spiritually blind human being who walked in total darkness, until the Lord Jesus Christ came and removed the scales from my eyes. He is a living and loving Savior Who wants to bring everyone into His marvelous light.

My fervent prayer is that you pray for those who don't know Jesus Christ as Lord and Savior. Please, let us not be too quick to judge anyone for what they believe, however strange it may seem. It was God's grace and mercy alone that brought you and me to Christ. Someone, somewhere, prayed for us, and we should do the same for others.

Chapter 3
My Grandparents' and Parents' Arranged Marriages

Some of Ma's personal stories would seem like fairy tales, but Ma was a lady who would never even whisper a lie. She was only sharing the Hindu way of life that she experienced, and we accepted her narrative without hesitation.

Hindus believe in arranged marriages. Even today, in certain parts of India and as well as in other nations, very young children are married off by their parents.

Ma was nine years old and Pa was twelve when their marriage was arranged by their parents, with a close friend of the family sealing the agreement. A measuring stick, yes, a stick was used in this important match. It was necessary that the boy be taller than the girl, so that dear old stick was required to perform this part of the marriage contract. When the two arranging parties agreed that the stick had faithfully performed its assigned task, it was carefully tucked away for another time, never to see the light of day until needed again.

Along with height, skin color was also taken into high consideration, always giving preference to a lighter shade. If darker, the party had to be financially well-off. In this case, Ma was of light skin, and Pa was a shade darker. However, that was okay because his father was a moneylender, and that helped seal the deal! Neither child was consulted in the matter of their marriage, nor did they see each other before the wedding day.

Of course, the Hindu pundit (priest) would give the best suited date for the marriage after he consulted with his religious books. For the wedding of this "child-couple," he would officiate in Sanskrit, speaking in Hindi only when he felt it was necessary. Honestly, no one understood what was said, as no one in my home understood Sanskrit.

Eighteen children were born of this union. Ma gave birth to my Uncle Ram at the ripe age of twelve. My mother was the first daughter and the third child of this big Sankar clan of seven sons and five daughters. Six children were lost at childbirth.

Upholding Hindu custom, Ma and Pa never walked physically side by side in all the years that they were married. Pa always walked in front, and Ma followed a few feet behind but near enough to carry on a conversation. In keeping with our tradition, my grandparents also never addressed each other by their name, as that was deemed to be disrespectful. Instead, they would say, "You hearing?" In other words, they wanted to make sure the other was listening.

My Parents' Arranged Marriage

My parents' arranged marriage took place under the watchful eyes of the same Hindu pundit who married Ma and Pa. My mom was fourteen, and my dad was fifteen. As with Ma and Pa, they had no say in the matter and never saw each other until their wedding day. However, the measuring stick wasn't necessary! My dad was over six feet tall, and his bride-to-be dwarfed him by at least five inches, so all was well.

Just three months after I was conceived, my teenage dad decided that he no longer wanted to be married. He missed his friends and wanted to play sports and go to the movies. He didn't want to have the responsibilities of a wife and child, so he sent my mother back to her parents.

My mother told me that before my dad sent her back home, he insisted that she eat a small, three-inch, raw fish to prove her love for him. When I heard this, I told my mother that I was glad it wasn't a cow or an elephant. I asked if my dad ate any of the fish, but he didn't. He just placed my mom's order and insisted that she leave nothing on her plate. She obliged.

My Birth

I was the first child of the first daughter of the Sankar family. My mother told me that I was born at home on a sunny afternoon with the local midwife waiting patiently to deliver me. This is where I grew up, and I am happy to say that my upbringing was not only in a house, but in a loving home.

In keeping with Hindu tradition, we were each named by the family's pundit. We treated him with great respect, bowing down at his feet whenever he visited our house to perform prayers. Hindus consider their religious leaders to be very holy, and so we bow down in reverence as a form of worship to them.

After the required eight day waiting period, my Ma consulted with the pundit about giving me a name. He consulted his religious books, looked at the stars, checked the positions of the moon and sun, and gave me the name, "Prema." I was also given a second name which I never cared for, and which the pundit said was "a hidden or secret name."

Prema, pronounced "Pray-Ma," is a Sanskrit and Hindi word. In English, it means, "Love," "Divine Love," or "Love on a Higher Form." At home, I was always called Prem, pronounced "Praim" (rhymes with same). I carried the last names of both my grandfather and my dad.

In our culture, having a male as the first child is always regarded as a high honor and preference. It is considered to be a greater blessing to the parents than having a baby girl. Amazingly, Ma told me that when I was born it was a special time for the family and my birth was celebrated with great joy.

She said that family, friends, and neighbors were invited to celebrate the occasion. A live orchestra performed for three days and nights, and people sang, danced, and enjoyed themselves. Food was freely given to the town, and even strangers were welcome to join in.

A sad note was that, during my birth and the three days of celebration, my dad was not around. However, my Ma and my family took me in and treated me as one of their own. There never was a time that I felt less of a daughter in this loving home. These very wonderful people always dearly loved this painfully shy child.

Growing up, as far as I understood, my aunts and uncles were my sisters and brothers, and Ma and Pa were my own parents. Our house was surrounded by fourteen lots of land with family houses on them, so we younger ones had a very large yard to play in. I was in a very safe and loving environment and had everything I needed, but in my heart, something was still missing.

CHAPTER 4
MY MA'S RELIGIOUS DEVOTION

Ma was a true, religious Hindu devotee. She was faithful, committed, and dedicated to what she believed in. As with most religious Hindus, prayers were tattooed on her hands and chest as a show of devotion to her gods.

Her day started in our temple at three o'clock every morning, before going out to work on the land. The first thing she did was pluck the best flowers from her beautifully cultivated garden to offer up in dutiful devotion as she worshiped. Some mornings, the rain came down in torrents, yet that did not deter her from gathering the flowers.

Rain or shine, Ma performed her duties without fail. She would place these flowers before the deities in the temple as she attended to them. The temple itself was a decorated place, brightly lit with dozens of small lights, and sparkling clean.

Hindu worship music and songs were often heard coming from a tape recorder inside the temple. Ma was a quiet lady by nature, but it was her habit to sing bhajans (religious songs) as she joyfully labored to fulfill her religious obligations. She was the first one up in the morning and the last one to go to bed at night.

Ma made sure to have many gods and goddesses, in all shapes, forms, and sizes, in our temple. There were little ones, medium sized ones, and big ones; some with a few heads and hands, some with many heads and hands, and some with many,

many heads and hands. We had a choice of which deity we wished to worship on any given day.

Shiva, with the cobra around his neck, was a favorite deity that was often worshiped in our household. Many large statues and several framed pictures of this god were displayed in the temple and throughout our house. Ma so reverenced her gods that she would actually wash the statues with cow's milk.

The Strange Smell

As a child, I clearly remember the time that one of my uncles had some friends visiting. He went beyond logical reason to own a forbidden tin of corned beef. When he tried to cook it, a very foreign smell revealed that something strange was going on in the kitchen. Very strange.

Pa led the investigation and quickly discovered the root cause. Addressing this daring act of treason, he sent the uncovered pot flying through the window, contents and all! That was the first and last time any attempt to cook beef took place in our house. The cow was a sacred mother, and no one ever again dared dispute that.

Worshiping the Sea

Nearly every Sunday, my eldest uncle would pack us up in his van like sardines and take us to the beach where we would spend most of the day eating and bathing in the warm waters. But first, we were warned not to enter the water until Ma had paid her devotions to the sea.

She would be the first to enter the water, fully dressed, with flowers and coins in her hands to give in worship to the sea. This assured us that no one would drown. After Ma was finished with her prayers, each one of us carried handfuls of flowers to throw into the water, asking the gods to bless and protect us.

Nevertheless, as a child I nearly drowned on at least three occasions. Sea water filled my mouth and it seemed like my eyes and ears too. Each time I resurfaced, I was so frightened. I believe God, in His great mercy, saved me for a time such as this.

CHAPTER 5
OUR NEIGHBOR "AUNTIE RUTH"

Usually when we returned from the beach, our neighbor Auntie Ruth, as we respectfully addressed her, would come over and ask Ma if we children could go to her house for milk and cookies. Auntie Ruth, her husband, and their daughter lived in a very small wooden house. They did not have many of this world's goods, but there was something different about them. They never had any prayers like ours but were the nicest people, and my family trusted them. We always enjoyed our visit.

Auntie Ruth taught us two choruses, "Leave Your Burdens Down by the Riverside" and "Keep in the Middle of the King's Highway." My Uncle Sone would quietly whisper that we shouldn't walk in the middle of the highway because we would get hit by a car.

She was a wise lady who never mentioned the Name of Jesus in her singing but referred to Him through these songs. Many years later, I would come to understand Who the King is and that the Lord used her and others to plant seeds of His Word in our hearts. How great is our God!

My Guru Uncle

One of my uncles had his house at one end of our property. He was a guru (a Hindu spiritual teacher or leader) who had his own temple and would often visit India. Sometimes, he would return accompanied by other gurus and a musical band, an arrival which would cause quite a commotion on Sankar Street.

First, the vehicles would pull up in front of his gate. From there, the procession would start. A bolt of red cloth would be hurled and unfolded for the visitors to walk on. It was the red carpet treatment, with the neighbors, who gathered to witness their arrival, each being given a piece of "walked-on-red-cloth" to keep for their spiritual advancement. Because these gurus were so highly esteemed, their walking on the red cloth was thought to make it holy and therefore much to be desired to attain spiritual growth.

The gurus, along with others deemed worthy, would then proceed slowly along the extended driveway toward the house. They were given the highest royal treatment, being fanned with peacock feathers. When they entered my uncle's house, only a chosen few would be allowed to join this select group.

My "Elder Sister" – My Mother

When I was four years old, my mother had yet another arranged marriage. More than sixty years later, I can still recall that day clearly. I cried and clung to my Ma with great fear when the wedding party was going to take me away with them. Because of my terrified reaction, it was agreed that they would come back for me at a later date. However, after the wedding my stepfather decided that he didn't want me to be a part of his family. In God's great providence, I was left with my Ma. Years later after I became a Christian, I saw the intervention of the hand of God in that stage of my life.

Yet, despite having a happy childhood and feeling loved by my family, within me something was not connecting. True, I was a painfully shy child, but that was not the reason. As I grew up, I realized that something was missing. There was a void that needed an answer.

When I was nine years old, I was told that my eldest sister, Shanmatie, was not, in fact, my sister but was my mother. I had no idea who I was really looking at every time she visited us. It was a good thing to know who my real mother was, but that still didn't fill the void in my heart.

Hindu School

Adjoined to a Hindu temple on the main road was a local Hindu school. Sometimes, classes were held in the temple itself. My aunts and uncles were all sent there, and so was I from the age of five to eleven. The school had strict standards, and we were expected to be diligent in our learning.

As a Hindu school, there were lots of religious activities. Every morning before classes started, we sang bhagans (Hindu devotional songs). As no English songs were allowed, we all sang in Hindi. We sang again before going for a ten-or-fifteen-minute recess, and then again after we returned. We sang and prayed before we went to lunch and sang after we returned from lunch. We sang a bhagan before and after our afternoon recess, and then we sang again and prayed before being dismissed for the day.

Now, it wasn't that we just sang bhagans. We sang these religious Hindi songs with great zeal and devotion as we gave worship to the Hindu gods and goddesses.

After my schooling there was completed, I went on to attend high school. Always having had a soft spot for the less fortunate and mistreated, it was my goal in life to become a lawyer so that I could help people.

CHAPTER 6
MY FIRST VISITATION OF THE LORD JESUS CHRIST

At the age of twelve, this shy Hindu girl had her first encounter with the Lord Jesus Christ. It was through the following dream:

I saw myself kneeling in a pew at the back of a small church, weeping profusely. In the dream, I had just been unjustly slapped and reprimanded by my grandmother and had run out of the house. Across the street, there was a small church (which was there only in the dream), and I had run into it. I was on my knees and sobbing heavily.

But then, I began to sense that someone else was in the room. As I gently lifted my head, I saw a statue of a man on the platform, painted in blue and white. Gradually, it began to shake from side to side and then slowly became a living person. He wore a long, blue and white gown and seemed to be about six feet tall. As I looked at Him in a mixture of awe and amazement, it was dropped into my heart: This is JESUS.

Slowly, He came down from the platform and walked towards me. He knelt beside me and put His arm around my shoulder. With His other hand, He wiped away my tears and said, "Do not weep, My child. Whatsoever you shall ask the Father for in My Name, you shall receive."

A deep calm came into my soul, and I felt so wrapped up in a blanket of peace. At the time, I did not realize the wonderful privilege I was being given through this experience.

Twenty years later, after I became a Christian, I came across these words in the Bible in John 16:23–24:

Whatsoever ye shall ask the Father in My Name, He will give it you.

Hitherto have ye asked nothing in My Name: ask, and ye shall receive, that your joy may be full.

Doubtless, in some Hindu homes, the Lord Jesus is added to the list of the millions of gods that are worshiped. Not in ours. In our home, the Name of Jesus was not whispered. We were Hindus, and that Name was forbidden.

That morning when I woke up, the urge to share my experience got the better of me. I said, "I dreamt Jesus." There was dead silence. No one showed any interest at what I said, nor did anyone care.

From then on – not another word! I knew that, as much as I was loved, I would be harshly rebuked, or even punished, if I were to say anything more. I myself didn't understand the profundity or the meaning of my dream, and I couldn't share it with my family.

However, it had happened. The Lord Jesus had visited me.

Many years later, after I was dramatically converted to Christianity, I realized that through this visitation Jesus was showing me that God is the living and true God. He is not an idol, nor should He be worshiped as one.

1 Thessalonians 1:9 says:

...and how ye turned to God from idols to serve the living and true God.

And John 4:23–24 says:

> *But the hour cometh, and now is, when the true worshipers shall worship the Father in spirit and in truth: for the Father seeketh such to worship Him.*
>
> *God is a Spirit: and they that worship Him must worship Him in spirit and in truth.*

The Lord Jesus Christ Rescues Me

Two weeks after my first experience with the Lord Jesus, I had yet another dream:

It was beginning to get dark, and I was late coming home from school. As I made my way through the back streets, I found myself passing by a cemetery. Suddenly, a long, black limousine drove up, and two men dashed out, heading straight for me. I knew that I was in grave danger and these evil men had come to kidnap me.

In a split second, I looked toward the sky and screamed, "JEEESUUUS!!!" Out of the clouds, the Lord Jesus Christ appeared, wearing a very white and shimmering long robe. He started to descend and stopped in a sitting position about three feet from the ground. The two men covered their faces with their arms, blinded by the dazzling brilliance of His robe.

The Lord Jesus extended His left arm, and I sat on it. Together, we went up toward the clouds. I was safe and secure in His arms. As a twelve-year-old child, I knew in my heart that when I was with Jesus those men could not harm me.

When I awoke, I stayed in my bed for some time, contemplating this wonderful dream. That day I didn't say anything to anyone. I knew that it was something I couldn't share.

This was the second time in my young life that the Lord Jesus visited me. However, it would be years before I understood what all this meant.

CHAPTER 7
MEETING MY DAD FOR THE FIRST TIME

When my parents' marriage failed, there was great animosity between my grandfather and my dad. Never having seen a picture of my dad, I had no idea what he looked like. I was told that he was very tall. It was not until I was close to being sixteen years of age that I met my dad for the first time.

One afternoon, while I was in English class in high school, my teacher informed me that I was dismissed for the rest of the day. When I came out of the classroom, an uncle and aunt were standing in the lobby. They informed me that someone was waiting at home to meet me. Knowing our marriage customs, I thought to myself, "Oh no! I am getting married for sure!"

As my uncle drove us in his car, my aunt combed my hair, making sure every strand was in place. She then whipped out a cosmetic case and powdered my face. I tried to ask questions, but there was mostly silence. I was on my way to finding out why I was being summoned so suddenly under these strange circumstances.

When we reached home, my family members were sitting there waiting for me. Among them was a very tall stranger with sharp features whom I did not recognize, with a lady sitting near him. My precious Ma greeted me with an embrace. Then, looking over to the tall stranger, she quietly said to me, "Prem, this is your dad." The man, who was over six feet tall, stood up and hugged me. The lady, who was his wife, also hugged me. And before I knew it, everyone was hugging me. Most of us were in tears.

It was a strange meeting. It seemed that streams of suppressed emotions within me were being released. I cried but tried to show myself brave. It was a surreal feeling that I was finally looking at this person whom, in the past, I had tried to envision. As we sat there, I shyly took glimpses of my dad and felt a deep sense of joy that I was finally able to meet him. He had remarried and brought his wife along to meet us all.

My father was also anxious to let me know that his marriage to my mom had failed because he wanted to enjoy life without any marital responsibilities. He said that during those days he spent a lot of time at the movies. He also thought it was best to keep away from the Sankar family. As he said to me, "I was young and strong and wanted to have my own way."

And in case you wonder about the fish episode, no, I didn't ask him why he insisted my mother eat a raw fish. I was just glad to have met my dad at long last.

And then I grew up fast – real fast.

CHAPTER 8
ARRANGED MARRIAGE AND TOTAL HEARTBREAK

For many years, I was terribly ashamed to share my testimony due to the stigma that divorce carries, especially among my own East Indian people. But, by God's grace, no longer. My past does not define me as a person, nor does it dictate my future. I am now free in Christ, and I am so thankful to Him! God has taken my broken life and is using it for His purpose and glory. Jesus has forgiven me and washed me in His precious shed Blood, giving me a new life. Now I call Him my Father and my God, and I totally belong to Him.

It is not my intention to share my experience with any malice or condemnation toward anyone who caused me pain. Neither is my story being told to offend anyone, not even my abuser. I could simply have written a paragraph or two on my horrific experience with domestic violence. However, this is a very important part of my life story, of my life's testimony, which I believe needs to be told so that others can be helped through it.

To those who are victims of domestic violence, I would like to say that by sharing my story I believe the discouragement in your life can be replaced with hope. So, be encouraged and strengthened as you read the outcome of my experience. There is a real, true, living God above, and He will make a way for you out of your difficulties. To God's glory, I am living proof of this.

You are greatly loved by God. If Jesus Christ can deliver me, He can, and most certainly will, deliver you too. Call upon the Name of Jesus. He will come to your rescue. Put your faith in Him, and He will fight your battles. I know because that is Who He Is. He is very kind, and He is on your side. He is justice and mercy to all who trust Him. Start seeking Him today and thanking Him in faith for helping you. Amen!

I grew up in a home where I never once had to cook. I liked school and enjoyed reading. Even though I was very quiet and hardly voiced my opinion, from a young age, God gave me a heart for the hurting and the defenseless. I even wanted to become a successful lawyer to help as many people as I could.

However, dreams and plans don't always work out our way, and in my case, the Lord worked everything out in a way that I could never have dared to dream or plan. Even though I experienced very terrible heartache on my pathway, the good news is that God has taken my helpless situation and horrible pain and has made them into a message of hope for others, and is using them for His glory.

In Hinduism, there is no dating or things of that sort. Normally, parents arrange marriages for their children. Even if you see someone you think you like, your marriage is still arranged for the sake of the family's "honor."

When my future spouse saw me, he said he liked me, and I thought I liked him too. So, without question, marriage was the next thing to do. It was as normal as breathing. After a while, my marriage was arranged. He was twenty-four. I had just finished high school, never had a boyfriend in my life, and was a very timid, seventeen-year-old teenager. As a teacher in school once said of me, "She wouldn't hurt a fly."

In keeping with our traditional upbringing, in my new home, I couldn't make eye contact. I was very aware of the rules and had to keep my head down while conversing, regardless of who I conversed with. In keeping with our traditions and customs, respect was absolutely required of me. I was trying so hard to do everything the right way, yet it was never good enough. I had no idea of the horror that awaited me when my spouse would become my abuser.

He was a first-generation Indian Trinidadian whose parents had migrated from South India. His mother once told me that her marriage was arranged when she was five years old and her husband was twenty-five.

The use of sacrificial animals was part of their worship. Entities were invited to enter certain members of the household, and then questions were asked by people seeking answers. His mother led this worship and would shake involuntarily as she spoke with a different voice, supposedly solving problems for those who took part in this ritual of blood sacrifice.

The marriage was a total tragedy. In the very first week of being in that house, my life became exceedingly stressful – a living hell. My abuser and his mother were very close, and she terribly resented me. I was ostracized. I soon found that this was the pattern for most of the wives in the family.

Unprovoked and violent beatings became a normal part of my married life. Sometimes, I was so severely beaten that I bled. I was kicked in the abdomen and violently raped with pillows placed over my face. My tormentor would drag me by my hair on concrete and wooden floors. Chunks of my hair were forcibly yanked from my head. Frequently, my scalp and head hurt so badly. Many times, I was choked. Several times, he hit me on my ear which punctured my Eustachian tube. Many times, I was left half-dead. Besides all these things, alcohol and marital unfaithfulness were part of his lifestyle.

One Sunday, I suddenly started to feel a sharp pain in my abdomen. As the hours went by, I could no longer stand upright but had to hunch over while clutching my abdomen. I felt nauseous and began to vomit. My abuser saw my condition and did nothing to help. On Monday morning, he went to work as usual, leaving me at home to fend for myself in that terrible condition.

A few hours later, I was able to contact someone who helped arrange a vehicle to take me to the hospital. After being examined, I was rushed into surgery with a "very close to rupture" appendix. I was told it was a close call. Once more, God had saved my life.

Few people could understand the intense mental pressure I went through during those days. I became suicidal and wanted to end it all but didn't have the courage to take the pills. There I was, raised in a loving and protective home, and then I had to live in that cruel prison. It was truly a horrific experience.

"What's a New Testament?"

On one of those awful evenings when I was alone in the bedroom, I came across a little red book. On the front cover were the words, "New Testament." Not knowing what that meant, I opened the book, curious to find out.

Just as I started to read it, he came in – very quietly and very unexpectedly. The angry look on his face, when he saw me trying to hide the little book in my hand, made me tremble in fear. Once more, and for no reason, I was his punching bag as he hit and knocked me aside.

He grabbed the little book from my hand and flung it through the window. Although I didn't know what a New Testament was, throwing that book out the window unaccountably troubled me. At first I felt sad, and then anger rose up inside me. In my despair, I told him, "You should never have thrown that book through the window! It would have been better if you had thrown me through the window! God will punish you!"

Daring to speak to him like that earned me some more severe beatings, this time with a wooden-handled broom. My arms were swollen and became black and blue all over. My mouth bled from his punches and slaps. But the worst thing was to see his mother standing there, encouraging him to beat me some more. My heart was crushed. And beat me more he did. Neither of them showed the slightest bit of sympathy for my suffering.

God bless his two younger brothers who would always try to help me out by saying something good to appease his temper, though to no avail. "Mind your business!" was his angry growl.

My abuser left early the next day for work. About mid-morning, I was surprised to see him slowly pulling into the driveway. As he came out of the car, I noticed his hand was swollen and bandaged.

As he was operating a machine, it suddenly malfunctioned, and his hand became caught. His five fingers were badly cut. That was the same hand he had used the evening before to fling the New Testament out through the window.

In spite of everything, I did all I could do to help him as his fingers healed.

Go to the Beach?

One day, my abuser suddenly insisted that we go to the beach. All day, the rain had been pouring and pounding, and I was puzzled that he wanted to go to the beach. Especially with me! But, in submissive obedience, I went along. Little did I know that he was planning to kill me.

The short end of the story is this: if the living God had not intervened, I would have died from "accidental drowning."

CHAPTER 9
HINDU MARRIAGE CUSTOMS AND TRADITIONS

My beloved reader, this may seem unthinkable to you, but unfortunately, this type of horrendous behavior goes on in countless homes. It is a normal Hindu custom that when a man gets married, he continues to live at his parents' house. His mother is always given first place, coming ahead of other family members. In many cases, his wife is placed in an inferior position somewhere down the line. In my case, I was so far down the line that it would have taken a high-powered telescope to find me.

As a new bride, I was shoved to the back seat of our car as the new bridegroom drove, while other family members occupied the front. Only those sitting in front were included in the conversation. It was my wifely duty to stay quiet until spoken to.

From a traditional Hindu perspective, the mother and son never come to terms with the fact that he is now married and has a wife. So, instead of a man leaving his father and his mother and cleaving to his wife, as the Bible says, he ignores or leaves his wife and cleaves to his parents.

That is so wrong. Why? Because parents are always to be loved, honored, and respected, but wives are to be treasured.

To my dear Hindu mothers and fathers who are reading this true story and are guilty of this behavior, never forget that the young lady who is brought into your home is someone's daughter, someone's sister, someone who was brought into your home to love you and your son. Show mercy and treat her well.

It is your motherly duty to train your children well and to teach your son to treat his wife with dignity. Just as you are a parent and have a mother, she has a mother too. Teach your son to love and show kindness to his wife. It will be a blessing to you and your family. Showing love and kindness is always a good and noble thing to do. I implore you to do that! I love you enough to say these things to help you, so please receive this word of kind counsel with an open and humble heart. It will change your life.

To the Hindu husbands reading this testimony, if you abuse your wife, if this is part of your lifestyle, I can only tell you that you need help. Ask God to change you from the inside out. He will show you mercy and help you to change. Your wife will respect the person you become.

Remember that your wife is loaned to you by the living God and she is not your property. She is not some object that you possess. She deserves to be treated as a human being, just as you would want someone to treat you, your own sister, or your mother. Your wife deserves your love. My dear brother, when you married your wife, she became your soul mate. She became one with you. When God looks at you, He sees both of you as one unit.

Do you understand that if you want a happy home, you must lead by example? Your wife is not a piece of trash to be tossed around like a football but is a soft and tender human being who, like you, was created by God Almighty. She needs to feel loved, treasured, and cared for by you. Take your rightful place and live with her in love, asking God for His help as you do your part in your marriage.

I love my Indian people, but some of our customs and traditions, especially those regarding our children, are very confusing and, in some cases, plain wrong. One perfect example is this practice that nearly ruined my life. If two young people see each other and think that they like each other, should they be forced into marriage? Where is the intelligence in that? These two people have a future ahead of them. Loving parents should help guide them into making the right decision for themselves, showing them that they are loved and trusted to do so.

Rushing them off to a forced wedding ceremony because of "family honor" is not the answer. In some cases, it's just like a death sentence, as it was in mine. Where is the honor in that? A forced marriage has nothing honorable in it. The parties may like or not like each other. It's part of life. However, to marry off a child or young person because that is "our culture" is destroying his or her future, no matter how well intended the practice may be.

My own grandmother was just nine, and my grandfather was twelve! Marriage? My mother was fourteen and my dad a mere fifteen years of age. Marriage? They were children, not pleasure objects. My beloved Hindu family, with all due respect, for the sake of all the young and innocent lives that have been and will be affected by this travesty, I stand up and speak up on their behalf. It is terribly cruel, and it is wrong. It must stop, and it must stop now!

Not always but still often, one's culture, customs, or traditions can be followed blindly, even if they are flawed. I see this in my Hindu upbringing, and I am certain that many of you will agree with me. Since we are brought up in a society where the majority of Hindu women hardly have a voice, sometimes we are treated in marriage as third class or "no class at all" citizens. Sometimes we are treated just as sexual objects to satisfy someone's passion. We have no choice but to go along with the very things that destroy us in the end. This must stop!

How very sad. It's something that absolutely needs to be changed. I am a living witness to the horror of some of these traditions, and I tell you now that the younger generation will rebel against these "laws" if things don't change.

Lastly, to my dear sisters who have been caught up in a situation like this, the same Lord Jesus Who rescued me and changed my life completely will make a way for each one of you. Call on Him!

A Prophetic Sign

Once in my abuser's house, as I was standing on thick, double mats doing dishes at the kitchen sink, one of his brothers walked in and quietly told me not to move. He had noticed the tail of a poisonous snake that had crawled under the mats. I was standing on the snake, unawares. Thankfully, he killed it. Looking back now, I believe it was a prophetic sign of the victory that would yet come in my future.

A little more than a year after, the marriage ended in divorce. If returning to my marital home was an option, I would have chosen to die first. This marriage produced only horrendous pain, and it was truly a death sentence. God allowed me to survive this terrible domestic violence and get away from all the physical, mental, and emotional abuse which nearly cost me my life.

Being so ashamed of the whole thing, for five years I said nothing to my own family regarding my experience. When I finally shared it with my precious Ma, she held me tightly and cried. She also chided me for not telling her, or anyone else, sooner.

Through it all and through a series of events, God made a way for me to escape from my deranged abuser.

CHAPTER 10
WARNING DREAM COMES TRUE

After moving to the United States, I worked at a record shop in New York City. One night, I dreamt that the store was robbed by two bandits who got away with three thousand dollars. That morning when I went to work, I shared my dream with the manager and secretary.

The very next day on the job, I was called into the manager's office. Pointing to a few small holes in the wall, he asked if I knew what they were. "No, sir," I replied, playfully sticking my finger into them. "What are these?" "They are bullet holes," he said. "Bullet holes?" I asked, without even thinking about my dream.

At that point the secretary spoke up, "Prema, your dream!" I screamed when I remembered it. They then explained to me, "Last night, two men came in with guns and robbed the store of three thousand dollars."

The Bible says that God gives gifts to His children, and I didn't even know that my gifts were being used. After my conversion to Christianity, I was taught that every gift that God gives to His people is to be used for His purposes in His kingdom. We are called to be like our heavenly Father, Who is the Father of lights, and allow His light to shine through us in this very dark world.

For our gifts to be used fully and properly, we must become born-again sons and daughters of the living God and live a life of consecration. (See the last chapter, "How to Receive Salvation.")

Searching for Meaning

I was still a naive young lady seeking for peace and fulfillment. In the process, my heart was broken as I looked to people for acceptance. What a fallen world we live in!

Because reincarnation is very much a part of the Hindu belief system, in my desperation I visited a hypnotist to learn about my past life and to find out why I was experiencing all this emptiness and pain. He told me that in my last life I had drowned in a river at the age of seven as I chased after a ball.

To think that he got paid for telling me these things is enough now to make me weep! Nothing he told me answered my questions or satisfied my hunger for fulfillment, but I meekly accepted my fate. "What a hopeless woman I am," I thought.

It was many months after I had invited Jesus into my heart that my eyes were finally opened to the truth. The particular Scripture that was quickened to my spirit at that time was Hebrews 9:27:

And as it is appointed unto men once to die, but after this the judgment.

For about six months after my conversion, I still couldn't understand or accept that we just die once. I shared my concern with someone, and she tried to help me understand, but at first it was difficult for me to accept. My response was, "Yeah, but..." I found out later that there is no "Yeah, but..."

"Yes and Amen!" The Bible is true, and God means what He says and says what He means.

CHAPTER 11
"YOU WILL LEARN TO LIKE HIM!"

At twenty-four years of age, I was living in Canada. My stepfather had moved his family there, and my mother had encouraged me to come too. They all lived together as a family, but I lived alone and worked in a bank.

One day, my mother announced that she was going to find me a husband. I was lonely but afraid to get married again. Her reasoning was that it was family custom and that "in our culture, it is not proper for an Indian girl to live alone like this." She reminded me that I was still young, insisted that I get married again, and was determined to arrange it.

Through the terrible beatings that I had endured in my first marriage, the Eustachian tube in my left ear was punctured. I had already undergone surgery, but the doctors said that my ear still needed medical attention. For a long time, I tried to avoid the additional surgery, but eventually, it had to be done.

It was a couple days after my second surgery. My head was in a huge, white bandage which had been circled several times around. I was just waking up from an afternoon nap, and was still quite dizzy, when I thought someone was sitting near my bed. Upon closer examination, with my eyes halfway closed, I caught sight of a man sitting on the chair in my room.

There I was, lying on a hospital bed in Toronto, Canada, with my head all bandaged up, and seeing my mother's choice of a marriage partner for me for the first time. With a big, jovial smile on his face, his first words to me were, "Hi Prrrreem!" However, I remained silent as I was at a loss for words. Under these strange and scary circumstances, who wouldn't be?

He came from a very good, wealthy Hindu Punjabi family, but I didn't want him to be my husband. When I told my mom so, that I believed he was a good man, but I didn't like him as a husband, she retorted in no uncertain terms, "You will learn to like him!" I never did. He never did. We never did. It might sound funny now, but that is the truth of the matter. Because I was recovering from surgery, the marriage had to wait for a few weeks. By then, I was back at my job. I worked until Friday but told no one that I was getting married the next day.

An Easter Baby

However, from this union was born a son whom I adore. On an Easter Sunday, my very kind Jewish doctor delivered my beautiful son at Mount Sinai Hospital in Toronto. A nurse handed me my precious baby with the words, "You have an Easter baby." An Easter baby? I had heard about an Easter bunny, but an Easter baby? I had no idea what she meant, except that it was a public holiday that day.

My precious son, Sanjay, has always been a great blessing to me, and to everyone. His first language was Punjabi, so when he was a child, it was quite comical to see my Ma's quizzical face when he talked to her. Ma knew Hindi, not Punjabi, so she would look to me, and I would translate whatever I understood. It was like going around the mulberry bush and carried quite a touch of humor!

My son is now married to a beautiful young lady, the first Christian in her Hindu family. His wife is such a great blessing to us all, and our family would not be complete without her. She is an answer to our prayers, and we love her dearly.

CHAPTER 12
JOURNEY TO THE HIMALAYAN MOUNTAINS

It was in the course of my second marriage that I went to India in my search for peace and truth, "looking for God." I had no idea that I was a lost sheep and that God, in His great love, had sent His Son, Jesus Christ, the Savior of the world, the Savior of all people, to die for my sins. It was Christ Who came looking for lost sheep – you and me.

Along with a few family members, I went on a pilgrimage to the Vaishno Devi Mandir, which is considered to be one of the holiest temples in Northern India.

The journey to the temple was physically and emotionally exhausting. After traveling for two days by car to reach Katra, the base camp at the foothills of the Trikuta mountains (which is a lower part of the Himalayas in the Union Territory of Jammu and Kashmir), there was yet more to go. I rode for five hours on horseback up the treacherous eight-mile path to the temple and then had to climb 740 steps.

The temple is in a cave at the foothills of the Himalayas. It is 5,200 feet above sea level. On both sides of the narrow tracks are steep precipices which drop thousands of feet down to the end of nowhere. Some pilgrims try to make the journey by foot, taking several days to complete it. One slip could lead to immediate death. It was a very difficult journey.

On the way to worship the goddess Vaishno Devi, my attention was captured by arresting sights. Children as young as six years of age stood in little huts and were worshiped as gods or goddesses. These young people hovered around in the hope of receiving some alms from the pilgrims. Older men traveled on the backs of younger men, but many refused to be carried. Instead, they crawled up the mountain on their bloodied knees with determination to reach the temple to worship their gods.

The belief that this penance and good work would take them to a higher plane in the next life motivated these religious and resolute people to keep going. However, many never make it to the top. In their frail, human frames, they die trying to get there, and their bodies just lie where they fall. To the Hindus, this is one of the noblest ways to die as it guarantees a much better future in the next life, one with less suffering when the soul is reincarnated.

One can hear the temple bells ringing from a distance. It is believed that they ward off evil spirits but are a pleasant sound to the gods and goddesses. It is also thought that the sound prepares the worshiper to clear his mind from all activity.

The temple is a cave of shrines, the main one being dedicated to the Hindu mother goddess Vaishno Devi. She is said to be an amalgamation of the three mightiest goddesses of power, knowledge, and wealth. Pilgrims have to literally crawl for about fourteen feet through a narrow opening and then walk in knee-deep, ice-cold water which flows from the Himalayan Mountains.

Thousands of devotees, in long lines, wait for their turn to pay homage to the gods and goddesses. I was one of them. Here I was, standing in the knee-deep, ice-cold mountain water for what seemed like an eternity, waiting for my turn to fall before one of my gods, a stone idol. My feet were cramped in the freezing cold water.

My Turn to Worship

Finally, my turn came. Here was the opportunity that I had been waiting for! Placing my offering of rupees as I prostrated myself, I began to pour out my heart before the mother goddess. To my shock and utter dismay, one of the temple guards came over to me saying, "Jaldee karo! Jaldee karo!" meaning, "Hurry up! Hurry up!" and motioned for me to move along. My turn was over.

I had barely started to worship. The whole process had lasted less than two minutes. At that moment, I felt cheated again. The long, tedious journey had turned out to be futile. However, in keeping with my religious beliefs, I tried to balance my thoughts by speculating that maybe, just maybe, in my last life I took too long to worship.

It took another five hours on horseback to descend from the Himalayas and three days to physically recover from the grueling trip.

My dear brothers and sisters in Christ, children of the living and true God, how grateful we should be that the Lord Jesus Christ shed His precious Blood on Calvary's Cross for all our sins! God is counting on us to tell the world about His love and sacrifice and to tell everyone that we do not have to crawl on our knees to obtain salvation.

How grateful we ought to be that we are saved, that salvation is a free gift, and that it came at such a great price! Thank God that when our Lord Jesus Christ hung and died on the Cross of Calvary, He paid the debt for the sins of everyone who will receive Him as Lord and Savior. It doesn't matter what race, tribe, nation, or culture we are from. When He hung on the Cross, we were all on His mind.

What a privilege it is to be born again of the Holy Spirit through the precious shed Blood of our Lord Jesus Christ! We must live for Him. Many Christians profess faith in the Lord but selfishly live for themselves. It is high time that we who call ourselves by that worthy Name, the Name of Jesus Christ, truly evaluate our lives in the light of the price that was paid by Jesus to save us from sin and from the devil.

My dear Christian brothers and sisters, to whom much is given, much is required. Our Lord Jesus Christ is coming back to take His people to be with Him. Let us help Him rescue His lost children by winning souls for Him. In this life, only that which we do for our Lord will count for all eternity. As I truly learned from the Word of God, we live only once. Let us not waste our lives by filling them with things of no eternal value.

CHAPTER 13
BATHING IN THE GANGES RIVER

The river Ganges, called Ganga Ma or Mother Ganges, is considered sacred and is personified as the goddess Ganga. The river is worshiped by Hindus who believe that bathing in it remits sins and helps to liberate the soul from the cycle of life and death. The waters are considered to be very pure and holy.

So, three days after my recovery from the journey to the Vaishno Devi Mandir in the Himalayan Mountains, I went on another pilgrimage with our family. This time it was to the Ganges River at Haridwar, an ancient city which lies at the boundary between the Indo-Gangetic Plain and the Himalayan foothills. It is regarded by Hindus as a holy place.

Worshiping the Cobra

Before getting on the boat which takes pilgrims to the bathing area, we joined a group standing around a sadhu (holy man) who was performing his daily ritual with a live cobra snake. There were several sadhus who were engaged in this same form of worship, each attracting his own audience. This is a common daily sight on the streets of India.

Some gave offerings of rupees as the sadhu used a flute to "charm" the cobra, which was looking out from a large basket. Milk and fruit are usually fed to the snake as part of the ceremony. Since snakes are a part of Hindu worship, this is a widely accepted and common practice.

Though, as a Hindu, I believed that the snake was one of my gods, I still made sure that there was enough room for me to start running should things get out of hand, worship or no worship. I would have been the first person to do a sprint in my Indian sari (the traditional garment worn by Hindu women).

Next, using a boat to get to one of the holy bathing areas, I fed the fish in the river, which are considered to be reincarnated human souls. It is thought that these fish could easily be some deceased and reborn family members, so no one is allowed to hurt or kill anything in the water. Of course, in line with my Hindu reincarnation beliefs, this was logical and natural to me.

At the temple of the goddess Vaishno Devi, thousands had lined up to worship, but there it seemed as if there were hundreds of thousands congregated along the banks of the Ganges. Among them were many foreigners who were dressed in full Indian garb and who, like me, were on a spiritual quest. As we spoke, I found out that there were engineers and doctors among the pilgrims who came to take part in the ritual. Emptiness knows no boundaries as the human heart seeks an answer to life. The quest is not just to exist, but to have real life.

Haridwar's chief object of pilgrimage is Har-ki-Pauri, which means "footsteps of god." Worshipers believe that a footprint of the god Vishnu is impressed into a stone at the bathing steps along the river and that the god Shiva also paid a visit here. The temples were packed to overflowing, the bells were ringing loudly every minute, and conch shells were blown at every turn.

Though large numbers of pilgrims gather annually in April, this was an extra holy time. It was the Kumbh Mela, a special festival whose exact date is determined according to Hindu astrology. It is held every twelfth year, and I was there in time to take my holy snan, the holy bath. Bathing in the Ganges River during the Kumbh Mela is considered to be a sacred act of cleansing the body and soul, and this festival attracts multitudes.

Even babies are "christened" or "baptized" in this river to cleanse their sins and protect them from evil spirits. A child is considered blessed to have undergone this ritual at the Ganges River. Adults bring the water of the Ganges back in containers, which is then used for other religious duties.

At the bathing area, hundreds of pundits and sadhus, many scantily clad, made their way to the front of the temple. They received much alms, adoration and worship from us devotees who followed. Since this was a once-in-a-lifetime trip for most, giving generously – very generously – to the pundits was considered to be another way that one could be ushered into a better karma.

Worshiping the Cow

Since cows are considered to be holy by Hindus (I suspect that's where the term "holy cow" originated), they, too, had their share of adoration. These docile creatures were decorated with ribbons of every bright color and were allowed to roam freely among the people. Musical bells around their necks chimed as they strolled. Many had religious symbols painted on them.

My dear reader, you may ask, "Did you really worship the cow?" Yes, dear reader, I really did worship the cow.

In my home, I did so through countless pictures and statues. At the Ganges River, I worshiped real, live cows. Unlike my careful plan to run from the cobra snake should it be necessary, I paid my respect to the cows by giving them homage when I encountered them. Part of this ritual was to place a mala, which is a garland of flowers, around the neck of at least one goddess cow, which I reverently did. I then prayerfully folded my hands and touched its head, honoring the cow for being such a beautiful goddess. I also fed the cows jalebi and ladoo (Indian sweets), which were purchased from the vendors at the riverbank.

The waters of the Ganges run very swift, and many have gone into eternity by drowning. When I went into the river, I dipped myself several times, holding on to the strong ropes which ran through the designated bathing area so as not to be swept away by the powerful currents. I must admit that I was happy to get out of the water, as it was freezing cold.

Unlike the story in the Bible of Naaman who dipped himself seven times in the Jordan River and was healed of leprosy, no matter how many times I dipped, and I can assure you that it was more than seven, I was still an empty shell of a human being. Hurting and not healed, I was still a struggling and wounded soul who felt so hopeless and worthless.

I thank my heavenly Father that when I came to know the Lord Jesus Christ, He not only dipped me, but He immersed me in His precious shed Blood. He is worthy of all praises and adoration. Praise His holy and most worthy Name!

I came out of the water of the Ganges River and felt no different. I was still so empty, unhappy, dissatisfied, and frustrated. "What is this?" I wondered. Something was sorely missing, and I couldn't put my finger on it. To make matters worse, I didn't know what to do about it.

On the long drive back to my family's home, which took us another two days, we were greeted by a blinding sandstorm. The sun was obscured, and the sky was dark. The sand got into the car, into our clothes, into our eyes, and into our ears. In order to breathe, we had to cover our noses.

Worshiping at the Golden Temple

Traveling through the state of Punjab, I also worshiped at the Golden Temple at Amritsar. I was pleased to visit this site as it connected me with the background of my dad's Sikh ancestors who originally hailed from there. The temple itself carries a lot of history, and it is considered by Sikhs to be the most holy place to worship.

In India, I traveled and visited many cities and states. I visited New Delhi and saw the revered tomb of Mahatma Gandhi, with its burning flame always lit. In Uttar Pradesh, I saw the famous Taj Mahal in all its splendor, one of the Seven Wonders of the World. I saw the beautiful Mughal Gardens in Srinagar, as well as spending time on a houseboat on Dal Lake in Kashmir. Haryana, Himachal Pradesh, Rajasthan, and Jammu and Kashmir each carry their own memories. Yet, I found no peace in my heart. How could I? I was unhappy and lost.

I had visited some of the most beautiful sites in the world but was still miserable. "What a karma!" I thought. Feeling very sad and hopeless, I was ready to rest my weary bones when we reached home. Tomorrow would be another day, another whatever. I just wanted to sleep for a long time.

CHAPTER 14
REFUSING TO BOW DOWN

Early one morning, a group of five religious women, who lived in a nearby temple, came to the house to receive alms. I was expected to bow down to them in worship and touch their feet with my hands. However, I felt an inward struggle and refused to bow down. It somehow bothered me to do so.

So, being defiant, I refused to prostrate myself at the feet of the first lady in line who presented herself before me. I could see her unbelievably shocked expression as she waited a few seconds more. Then she got really angry. She lifted one of her feet straight toward my face so that she could be worshiped.

With anger and frustration spewing out of my soul, I felt like taking her foot and spinning her around. Such was the state of my hopeless and hurting mind. "What is THE TRUTH???" my poor, empty heart cried.

In the eyes of my family, I was being disrespectful and insulting. They were hurt and thought I was rudely out of order.

After that incident, whenever this group visited the house, the leader would steer clear of me. I had no problem doing the same. I was so tired of living this empty, meaningless religious life and going around in circles.

Looking back, I realize that no matter how hard we try, no matter what we have or don't have, no matter where we go, no matter how many risks we take, we will always be lost and unfulfilled as long as we run after empty things. I was running after gods that didn't exist! They were gods of stone and wood, marble and clay. They were painted, hand-crafted objects which were called gods and goddesses. I was satisfying my eyes with places and things, but that was not the answer to my broken life and hurting, unfulfilled soul. Inside, I was an empty and dead shell.

Adding to my pain, my marriage was as empty as my heart. When my son was two years of age, his dad and I went our own ways. Our separation had started before we ever got married. There were other serious contributing factors which added more difficulties to this already forced and broken marriage.

However, I am quite pleased to report that my son's dad is now remarried with a good wife and two fine boys. His marriage was arranged by his parents, and from what I know, they love each other. I am truly and sincerely very happy for them.

I am also happy to report that even after I became a Christian, Sanjay's grandparents would always visit us in Canada during their regular summer trips from India. They wept because of the marriage breakup and remained very cordial and kind to me. They always expressed their love for me and said that I was always welcome to visit them whenever I came to India. I was also told that I would always be regarded as their daughter-in-law. They accepted the failure of the marriage as past karma.

From Barren to Six Children

In India, I met a family member who had been childless for the eight years of her marriage. I told her, "The next time I visit India, you will have a child." And so it was! Lo and behold, by my next visit, this dear lady had given birth to a child. After the birth of her sixth child, I sent her another message, with a smile, "You can stop now!"

Round Three. Will It Ever End?

Back in Canada, working full-time and raising my son as a single parent kept me very busy. When my son was five years old, I went through another difficult marriage which was arranged for me. This one was annulled very soon after it began, as the previous wife was still part of his life.

In the midst of my turmoil, God intervened again in my life, this time by sending me help through Mrs. M. C. and her wonderful family. They were so kind to me, a total stranger, and did everything they could to ease my pain. Their love was greatly displayed, and I will be forever indebted to them.

However, the emotional and mental pain that I experienced drove me to the brink. I was lost – so lost – and could not find my way. By the time I was thirty-one years old, I had three arranged and failed marriages. My heart was broken. I was a total basket case – searching, confused, and bewildered, with more questions than answers.

Bipolar Depression

I had already been through so much pain in my young life. This was just too much. I fell into deep manic depression and was a walking dead woman. Days went by without my getting out of bed. I wouldn't brush my teeth or comb my hair. I didn't know how to smile. There was total darkness in me and around me, as when day turns into night. I had no desire to live and thought of just committing suicide, once and for all. According to my Hindu beliefs, I would be reincarnated and would return in a different form.

However, my sweet son's innocence and his pleading and beautiful face seemed to stop my thoughts of suicide. My precious six-year-old child would sit and weep with me, holding my hands and saying, "Mom, it will be all right. I will take care of you." How I give the Lord thanks for my priceless child!

Oh, the pain of just living! Just thinking of getting up was a burden and a task. Everything around me was black and gloomy, and I had no hope of ever recovering. I felt totally doomed. My mind was hurt, my emotions were confused, my body was tired, and nothing made any sense at all. I had no hope, none whatsoever.

"I Dare You to Strike Me Dead!"

One day, in my confused and crazed state of mind, I pointed my fists to the sky, and in great anger I shouted to whoever I thought was up there, "I am a good person! Why are You doing this to me? I don't want to live! I dare You to strike me dead!" In my totally dark state of mind, in my senselessness, in my pride, in my sinfulness, in my madness, this piece of clay was challenging my Potter, my loving and wonderful Creator Whom I did not know.

I had a lot of religion, enough religion to sell, religion up to my neck, but I didn't have the living and true God in my heart. I would soon find out that I wasn't as wonderful as I thought I was. Far from it. I was a very proud and a very lost sinner who was headed for hell and who deserved to go to hell, yet I thought so highly of my own pitiful and vain self. How quick we are to blame God for our own foolish doings.

Thank God that He is so merciful that He doesn't strike down us puny mortals when we exhibit our extreme folly by our ignorant and unspeakably stupid actions. What mercy! What love!

CHAPTER 15
CONVERSION – TRUTH REVEALED – JESUS IS THE ANSWER

"Jesus has come and my cup's overrun,
O say, but I'm glad!"

Despite all my religious good works and rituals, I was still a total wreck. Nothing worked. I was so lonely, still searching for meaning, and my life continued to spiral downwards. My pain and emptiness were so great that I felt hopeless and sometimes numb.

The Hindu pundits told me that I was paying for sins committed in my past lives. They said that I had to complete a certain amount of suffering and punishment in this life for things I had done in my previous life and birth cycles. It was not a difficult thing for me to accept because as far as we were concerned, the pundits knew everything. We thought that they had attained a greater level of spirituality, were more god-conscious, and therefore were more in tune with the inner-self than the rest of us. What I could not deal with was the emotional and mental pain. I was alive, yet only dreadfully existing.

Oh, how I thank the God of grace and mercy for the day He looked down from His holy heaven and saved me from the pit of eternal hell!

"Jesus paid it all,
All to Him I owe;
Sin had left a crimson stain,
He washed it white as snow."

To the eternal glory of the living God, this is my amazing and miraculous conversion story:

Leaving my aunt's apartment in Brooklyn, New York, where Sanjay and I were staying, I don't know why but I found myself on a train heading into Manhattan. It was a cold and blistery Saturday morning, and a blizzard was on the way. I wandered around aimlessly for a couple of hours, wearing only a light coat. I felt numb and had no concept of how cold it really was.

Passing by a small restaurant, I noticed stacks of free newspapers against the showcase. I can't clearly remember if I got myself a cup of tea, but I picked up a newspaper and headed for the subway station. When I reached home, my son was playing with his cousins. Barely greeting anyone, in my sad and sorry state, I headed straight for the bedroom. I had no idea that, within minutes, my life was about to change forever!

Plunking myself down on the bed and angrily opening the newspaper, I flipped it from page to page. But then, all of a sudden, I reached the church section. My eyes were drawn to a particular advertisement, "Zion House of Worship," which included an address and telephone number.

The only way I can express what happened next is to say that I felt as if I was "arrested." Something within me "boomed" three times, "Call the church! Call the church! Call the church!" I thought to myself, "I am a Hindu. Why should I call this Christian church?" However, I felt compelled to dial the number, even though I thought that I might slam the telephone down before it was answered. But our awesome God had other plans. The telephone was answered by the pastor – who turned out to be a former Hindu! It was a divine appointment.

I was crying uncontrollably, literally bawling, while trying to tell him that I needed help. He listened sympathetically, paused, and then told me that he knew someone who could help me and that he would introduce me to this person the next day. He invited me to meet with him and his wife the next morning at church and gave me directions how to get there. Before he hung up the telephone, he prayed for me. To this day, I don't remember what he said in that prayer.

The next morning, New York was blanketed with a terrible blizzard. The buses were getting stuck all over the city. My well-meaning aunt tried to discourage me from leaving home and "going out in that weather." I remember replying to her, "I need help. I have to go." I got lost all over New York City, despite having lived there years before. My mind was so disoriented. When I finally reached the train stop, an elder from the church was waiting to drive me to the place where we would be meeting.

Zion House of Worship met in the basement of the pastor's humble home. This dear man of God, whom I had talked with on the telephone, came to me and introduced himself and his wife. It was a small gathering, mostly ladies. They were dressed in their beautiful Indian saris. Each one lovingly embraced me. The ladies hovered around me, wanting to make my visit comfortable.

The service started with the most beautiful worship music. Those present reverently bowed their heads and sang to God from their hearts. I looked around, stunned to see Indian people worshiping in a way that was so different from anything I had ever known. I had never seen such a thing before, not with my own Indian people. This was all new to me.

As the pastor began to preach, he told the story of his conversion from Hinduism to Christianity. His mother had been bitten and killed by a cobra snake that his family was worshiping in their home in India. Shortly after this tragedy, missionaries led him to the living and true God.

He then preached a message that I had never heard before. As I listened, the light of God began to dawn upon that pit of darkness in my very lost soul. As the Bible says in 1 John 1:5:

> *This then is the message which we have heard of Him* [Jesus], *and declare unto you, that God is light, and in Him is no darkness at all.*

The pastor preached how the Son of God, by the Name of Jesus Christ, came into this world because God, His Father, had sent Him. I heard how Jesus Christ gave His life on the Cross of Calvary to save the world from sin. I heard how He was nailed to a Cross, bled, and died so that even the worst of sinners could find hope. I had always thought that I was so good, but God was revealing the true condition of this proud, wretched, and lost sinner's heart.

I also heard that Jesus was the only way to heaven. Now *that* I could not understand. My precious Ma had always told us that there are many roads to God and that no matter which road we took, as long as the heart was clean, we would still end up with God. What was I hearing now? I was puzzled. Surely my precious Ma would never lie to us! Why was I now hearing something different?

As I continued to listen, I heard that God offered us a free, priceless gift when He gave the world His Only Begotten Son, Jesus Christ. I saw people weep as the pastor preached. They seemed to be genuinely touched by what he was saying, although I myself didn't quite fully understand it all.

However, I felt sorry to know that someone was nailed to a Cross. For me.

At the end of his preaching, the pastor gave an invitation

for me to receive Jesus Christ into my heart. He asked if I would like to give my life to Him, to the God Who had died for my sins and for the sins of the whole world. He explained that this Person, Jesus, died and was raised from the dead by the power of God, and that this Person, Jesus, is alive. He said this Person, Jesus, is the living God. He said that this same Jesus could wipe my past slate clean and help me by giving me a new beginning. Oh, how I needed help and a new beginning!

The pastor repeated that if I would like to ask Jesus to come into my heart, to please come forward.

Although I didn't fully understand everything I had heard, I felt a tugging in my heart to respond. After all, I had never before heard of anyone dying for my sins.

I went forward. As the pastor led me in a prayer of repentance for all my sins, and as I received the Lord Jesus Christ as my Lord and Savior, something happened to my heart. Though it was terribly cold outside, my heart was filled with a warmth, peace, and joy that I had never known before.

That cold and wintery day in 1984, without really understanding what I was doing, in faith I gave my life to the Lord Jesus Christ. I made a choice, in faith, to believe that God loves me and that He sent His Only Begotten Son, Jesus Christ, to die for me on the Cross. In faith, I made a choice to believe that Jesus rose from the dead and is alive forevermore.

How wonderful it is to know that this God is the living God, the true God! One God. And this true God loves you! And me!

Weights Roll Off! Scales Fall Off!

At the very instant that I committed myself to the Lord Jesus, I felt as if tons of weight rolled off my back. I know now that those tons of weight were the burden of my sin that I carried. I finally felt light and clean. The Blood of Christ had cleansed my very sinful heart. Oh, how I thank You, Lord!

At the same time, I also experienced the remarkable sensation of scales falling off my eyes. For the first time in my life, it seemed as if I could see more clearly. Everything looked new and bright. The leaves were greener, the sky looked bluer – even dogs looked pretty! I felt so clean, so calm, so peaceful. I was indeed a new creation in Christ, born from the Holy Spirit of God. A spiritual rebirth had taken place in my life, instantly! I was ushered from total darkness right into the wonderful and delivering light of Jesus Christ. I felt so free from the religious shackles that had me bound. What freedom!

Sometime later, while reading the Holy Bible, I came across the story of the conversion of the Apostle Paul. After Ananias prayed over him, the Bible says in Acts 9:18:

And immediately there fell from his eyes as it had been scales: and he received sight forthwith, and arose, and was baptized.

I now understand why I had believed in reincarnation and why I had thought that I was to be recycled many times over. Scales had covered not only my eyes, but also my heart. Dense spiritual scales.

The Bible says that the devil is the inventor and father of lies, the greatest of deceivers. However, JESUS intervened and revealed His truth to my sinful, hopeless, crushed, and broken heart. He wants to do the same for you.

JESUS CHRIST IS TRUTH! HALLELUJAH!

The pastor did say that he would introduce me to someone who would help me. He did not lie to me – he introduced me to the Lord Jesus Christ Who has been my life, my strength, and my helper ever since that memorable day!

Chapter 16
My Precious Ma Didn't Lie, but She Was Sincerely Wrong!

My precious Ma, whom I dearly love, had told me that there are many ways to heaven. My precious Ma would never lie. She told her family what she thought was true. She was sincere, but I found out that even my precious Ma was sincerely wrong.

In the Holy Bible, the Lord Jesus Himself said in John 14:6:

I am the way, the truth, and the life: no man cometh unto the Father, but by Me.

Who are we to tell the Lord Jesus Christ that He is wrong and that He is a liar? God forbid!

My dear friends, yes, Jesus really did come into my heart through His Holy Spirit. He changed my heart and gave me a new life. He touched me! He washed me in His precious Blood, threw my past into the sea of forgetfulness, cleaned up my life, and gave me a brand-new beginning. Glory to God! I am amazed to know that, in spite of all my horrible sins, Christ saw my helpless state and shed His Blood for me. Mercy is His holy Name! How Great is our God!

Dear reader, I was a great sinner who needed a great Savior and who found my Deliverer in the Lord Jesus Christ. Something happened to this poor, sinful and desperate idol worshiper. At the age of thirty-two, I was touched by the holy and mighty hands of the living God!

The day I gave my life to the Lord Jesus, a fountain filled with tears of joy and gratitude was released from my inner being. To think that He loved me so much that He was willing to die for me! I was so touched and moved by this revelation of truth that, from that day, I still marvel at this kind of divine, pure, holy, and perfect love.

Also, the love and acceptance that were given to me through those true Christian people, in that humble basement church, helped me to want to live again. Among all the lovely people whom I met there were members of the Thangavelu family. I was so encouraged by Ruth, my beautiful sister in the faith, and by her mom, whom everyone called Amma and who has since gone home to be with the Lord and to receive her reward. Sister Ruth and her family still pray for me and my family after all these years. I thank God for that kind of unselfish love.

The pastor and congregation were from South India. Looking back, I thought how ironic it was that, in my first marriage, I was nearly killed by a man with South Indian roots, but here the Lord used that same people group to introduce me to the Life-Giver, Jesus Christ! God is so amazingly good!

Most of all, JESUS came into my heart and changed my entire life, for which I am so very and eternally grateful.

One Single Convert in Five Years – Me!

I found out that the pastor faithfully advertised the church service in the newspaper for five years...and that I was his only convert! Pastor Samraj had no way of knowing just how many souls he was reaching when the Lord saved me through his ministry. He was touching generations! I am so glad that he didn't pack up and walk away when he saw no visible fruit during those five years.

I want to add here that if you are a minister of the Gospel, and if you are discouraged because nothing much seems to be

happening through your ministry, please, I urge you not to give up. Take heart and stay faithful to the Lord. Though it can be very trying sometimes, never give in! You might just be on the verge of your breakthrough. God sees your labor of love that you offer up in His Name.

If, during those five years, Pastor Samraj had given up advertising the church services, I would not be here today. He stayed faithful to God, walked in the love of God, and trained his congregation to do the same. I personally witnessed this.

So, with God's help, be a good and faithful leader, and the Lord will reward you. Some may despise you, but never mind that. Your reward comes from the One Who assigned you. The Lord is your strength, your deliverer, your high tower. He is the victorious God Who flies high His everlasting banner!

CHAPTER 17
"YOU BECAME *WHAT*???!!!"

That Sunday morning, I left home in a state of deep depression and confusion. Rejected, forsaken, suicidal, depressed, and oppressed by the devil, I was dying deep inside and felt utterly miserable. I had no direction in life and had nothing to offer anyone, except my woes.

When I left church, New York City was still in the midst of the big winter blizzard. The wind was howling, and it was still freezing cold. But I felt so different! A supernatural peace ruled my heart. I saw beauty in everyone and everything, even in the coldness of the snow. God had given me new spiritual vision, and all the scales were gone. At last I could truly see!

I returned home late in the afternoon and didn't have to say a word. For the first time in a very, very long time, I was smiling. My aunt greeted me at the door and seemed puzzled. The first thing she haltingly said to me was, "What, what happened to you? Your, your face looks different."

I felt very peaceful but didn't know that my face showed it. Oh, to be at peace, the peace that I had longed for, the peace that I had searched for. Finally, the Prince of Peace, Jesus Christ, had taken His rightful place in my heart and life.

Still standing at the door, I calmly replied, "I became a Christian today." Her face contorted with shock and fury, and in abject horror she shouted, "You became *what*???!!!"

I could see her anger and disappointment because of what I had done. In her mind, I had become a traitor to my Hindu beliefs and had betrayed my own people. "I was born a Hindu, and I will die a Hindu!" she angrily shouted, her face turning red. Her hair just about curled.

In spite of her reaction that day, I just wanted to hug my precious six-year-old son and spend some much-needed quality time with him. He was beyond overjoyed to see his mother smiling and happy! I looked at my precious son's face and saw how happy he was to see his mom happy. I saw a change in him before my very eyes. Before that, because of my painful and confusing life, he was withdrawn and sad. Now, he was so bubbly and full of laughter. Oh, it was so very good to see my child just being a happy little boy!

The light and love of Jesus Christ, my Lord and Savior, had come into my heart, and I was finally at home – at rest and at peace. My search had ended. I had found the answer to my futile, broken life. Thank You, my Father!

How Great Thou Art!

The next Sunday, I was back at church, this time with my son. We were treated like royalty. The members were constantly praying for me and my loved ones. As we worshiped, I was shown how to read and sing the hymns, as I didn't have a clue how to do so. The very first song I learned as a Christian was "How Great Thou Art!" How appropriate! I will always have a very special love for this hymn and will forever continue to discover how very great my God is.

Water Baptism and My Two Dollar Gown

Six weeks after my glorious salvation experience, I was water baptized by the pastor and elders at Zion House of Worship in Queens, New York. A couple of days earlier, as I looked for a decent dress for my baptism, a store owner sold me a beautiful white gown with a small, white, dainty, flowered jacket. As he shared the story behind it, my heart was touched.

The outfit was ordered for a bride who never made it to the altar. So, it was taken down to the basement and left there for three years. He ended with, "I just brought it back up this morning and will let you have it for two dollars." This beautiful dress was still in its protective plastic case. It was clean, brand new, and fitted me just right.

Meanwhile, God had already started to work in my aunt's heart. She came to see me get baptized, and yes, as I got out of the pool, she was the one holding my towel. To God be all the glory! Hallelujah!

What a change our Lord Jesus makes in our lives! It reminds me of what David the Psalmist said in the Scriptures in Psalm 30:11–12:

Thou hast turned for me my mourning into dancing: Thou hast put off my sackcloth, and girded me with gladness;

To the end that my glory may sing praise to Thee, and not be silent. O LORD my God, I will give thanks unto Thee for ever.

My Best Friend

You are my Friend, Whom I can trust,
You saved my soul when I was lost.
You saw my tears, You felt my hurt,
You took my pains, You gave me mirth.

In You, I can truly find rest,
Especially when I go through my tests.
I can call upon Your Holy Name,
You Who love me so, You Who bore my shame.

A Friend to me, You are indeed,
A Friend Who knows my every need;
A Friend Who took my burdens and pain,
A Friend through Whom Eternal Life I gained.

Down in the valley, with all my cares,
I can cast my burdens, without any fears –
For You are everywhere;
A Friend Who is faithful, a Friend Who is dear.

When the weight of life feels heavy
And there is darkness all around,
You gently take my hand in Yours,
And in my heart, You put a song.

You are my Redeemer, You are my Lord,
You are my Savior, You are my God;
You are so gentle, You are so true,
You are my Best Friend,
What would I do without You?

I love You, Lord Jesus!!!

–Prema Pelletier

CHAPTER 18
AN ANGEL COMES TO MY RESCUE

A couple of months later, while flying from New York to Toronto, I was seated next to an intelligent-looking, well-groomed gentleman. Being so happy and proud of my newfound faith, I shared that I was a former Hindu and had recently become a Christian. He wanted to know more about Hinduism, so I explained a few things to him.

Even after the plane had landed, we continued our conversation. As he started to question me about the Bible, I wasn't able to answer him, having just become a Christian myself. All I knew was that I was told by the pastor that I was now a born-again Christian and everyone needs to be ready because Jesus is coming back soon.

Right out of nowhere, another well-groomed gentleman edged his way into our conversation. He looked at the man and simply said, "She's right. You have to be born again to go to heaven. Jesus died for your sins, and He is coming back soon." The first man excused himself and hurriedly left.

I thanked my rescuer, but before I knew it, with a great smile, he seemed to simply vanish before my eyes. I couldn't see him anywhere, and I didn't know where he had gone. I believe he was an angel sent from the Lord to help me. Thank You, Lord! Thank you, angel!

Brother Wolf Drops By

The Lord provided a place for my son and me to live, and my job was less than five minutes away. I was a baby Christian and had just begun to read the Bible.

Unexpectedly, a pastor, whose church I had visited, came to my home, uninvited and with evil intentions. When I understood his motives, I demanded that he leave at once and became angry with Christians and Christianity. I thought to myself that if this is Christianity, then I didn't want any part of it. At that time, my understanding of my new faith was very limited.

There will always be wolves, smartly dressed up in sheep's clothing.

However, there will also be true Christians. Yet, even a true Christian is not perfect and will sin and fall short. Thank God that, in our fallen state, in Jesus' Name, when we sincerely confess our sins to God and repent, which means turning away from our sins, we are forgiven, no matter who we are or what we have done. Jesus came to forgive and rescue us if we humble ourselves, forsake our sin, ask for His mercy and forgiveness, and in like manner, also forgive all those who have sinned against us. I am so glad for such a Savior, or else where would I be today? I know the answer to that question. I would be in the deepest part of hell, burning in hellfire for all eternity!

Dear reader, do you know this wonderful Savior? Many say, "I know Jesus."

The greater question is, "Does Jesus know you?" The Bible says you must accept Him into your heart and acknowledge your sinfulness.

But, at the time of this unfortunate experience, I was at a loss for words. Because of it, for several months I went back to living the way I did before. However, the Lord had great mercy upon me and sent a dear lady, a bank customer, who invited me to attend church with her. I shared what had happened, and she was so sorry and apologetic to me for the whole incident. I visited her church with her and ended up staying there for nearly eight years.

A Leak in the Ceiling?

During the few Sundays that I attended church in New York, I noticed that some people lifted their hands toward the ceiling during worship. I was puzzled but never asked why. I soon learned at this new church that raising one's hands is a form of reverent, heartfelt worship.

I had actually thought that the people were pointing to the ceiling to tell everyone else that there might be a leak up there, and that when the pastor pointed to the ceiling, he was acknowledging that he was aware of the fact.

The very idea! A newborn baby in the things of God.

Baptized with the Holy Ghost and Fire!

About two and a half months into my new walk with the Lord, while in worship during an evening church service, I stood in the pew with my hands lifted up, weeping with gratitude that God had saved me from going straight to an eternal hell. The sermon was on the Baptism of the Holy Spirit, and I heard people speaking in a different language, what the Bible calls "speaking in tongues." A hunger stirred within my heart. I then quietly asked the Lord to "please give me what these people have."

As I stood there, in His infinite mercy, my Lord Jesus met with me again. I saw and felt a ball of fire, as big as a handful, just zap me on the top of my head. A strange language started to form within me and before I knew it, I was speaking it out. God had given me my prayer language.

No human hands were laid on me at that moment. That night, Jesus baptized me in the Holy Ghost and fire. By God's grace, I have been shouting ever since, and the fire has been burning ever since! Hallelujah! Thank You, Jesus!

In the physical realm, when a house is on fire, people shout for one reason or another. Well, this "house" is on Holy Ghost fire! Some well-meaning Christians (bless their hearts) have tried to silence my shout, saying that it is too loud. No, sir! Not loud enough, dear child of God! The Holy Ghost and Fire Baptizer, Jesus Christ, has set this house on fire and by His grace, I expect to shout right until the day He says, "Come up hither." Besides, if you came from where I came from, you would be shouting too!

We need to appreciate what Christ has done for each one of us who claim to be His son or daughter. Yes, there is a time to shout and a time to keep silent. However, that should not stop us from glorifying the Lord with shouts of praise. Remember when some of you yelled at the top of your voice at a sports game...?

Watch Out – Bullets Are Flying!

Canadian winters are very cold and snowy, but with my newfound faith, my son and I braced the weather and went to church. Sometimes, I would get a ride to church, but for the most part, since my car was still in New York, my son and I took a bus, a train, and then another bus to get there. It was such a pleasure to sit and hear the Word of God being taught.

One very cold night after a late service, as a few of us were being driven home in the church bus, the window where I was sitting was totally shattered, with the broken glass falling on my lap. Because it was winter and I was wearing a thick coat, I was spared from getting hurt. It turned out that two drunk young men were shooting guns from an apartment balcony window.

When the police came and looked at the whole scene, one said to me, "If the bus were going any slower, you would have been shot in the head." One more time, God spared my life for His glory. I met those two shooters in court, reminding them that they had a life ahead of them, and telling them that I forgave them. Sadly, they had once known the Lord but fell away. They promised me that they would get back into fellowship with Him.

CHAPTER 19
THE GOSPEL – AN OFFENSE

Being so full of the joy of salvation in my new faith, I shared the Gospel wherever and whenever I could. I shared it with other employees and customers at work, not leaving out the bank manager. She was quite friendly with me and didn't seem to mind. However, as time went on, the Gospel turned out to be an offense to her. One Thursday, she called me into her office, ordering me "not to talk about this Jesus anymore in this bank!" As a new Christian, I was devastated, but the Lord sent me a beautiful Christian couple from church to encourage me. They even brought me a large bouquet of flowers.

The very next day, the manager received a call from our head office, informing her that she was being transferred to another branch. Within eight days, she was gone. I remained at that branch for another four years. The new manager allowed me to share the Gospel to my heart's content. He told me that, though he didn't share my beliefs, he respected my convictions.

Psalm 23 in the Face of a Pointed Gun

During my years in the bank, I experienced several robberies. One afternoon, coming back from my lunch hour, I heard the words, "This is a hold-up! Everybody down!" And down we all went! Fear grabbed hold of the employees as the robber pointed his gun at us. I was the one closest to him. Still on the floor, little by little, I started to inch myself away as he opened the tellers' cash drawers and stashed the money.

After the robber left, my fellow workers told me that they had heard me whispering, *"Even though I walk through the valley of the shadow of death, I will fear no evil, for Thou art with me. Thy rod and Thy staff, they comfort me."*

The Lord's presence in the midst of that situation truly comforted me. That line is from Psalm 23, one of my favorite psalms. All six verses are so rich with meaning:

The LORD is my shepherd; I shall not want.

He maketh me to lie down in green pastures: He leadeth me beside the still waters.

He restoreth my soul: He leadeth me in the paths of righteousness for His Name's sake.

Yea, though I walk through the valley of the shadow of death, I will fear no evil: for Thou art with me; Thy rod and Thy staff they comfort me.

Thou preparest a table before me in the presence of mine enemies: Thou anointest my head with oil; my cup runneth over.

Surely goodness and mercy shall follow me all the days of my life: and I will dwell in the house of the LORD for ever.

Thank God for His Word of comfort that helps us when we are in difficult circumstances.

Salvation of Three People Through a Dream

One night, I had a dream about a particular family of three who were bank customers. Paying them a visit, I shared the love of Jesus with them. They became Christians and joined the church I attended.

Crazy for Jesus

Several years ago, I met with one of my previous bank supervisors, Maggie. When I witnessed to her about Christ, she grabbed hold of her son's hand and said, "Let's get out of here. This woman is crazy!" Five years later, the Lord impressed upon my heart to telephone her. By then, she had left Canada and was living overseas. She started to weep and told me that she was so relieved to hear my voice. There was a serious family situation, and she needed some counsel. She said that for several months she had been trying to find me.

After my friend had poured out her heart to me, I encouraged her to give herself to the Lord, as He really is the only One Who can give us the help we sorely need. This time, Maggie gladly said "Yes" to the Lord as we prayed on the telephone.

Our ministry had the privilege of baptizing her in water when she visited Toronto. Her's is a story of true conversion. Today, she loves the Lord with all her heart and serves Him fervently. Now she, too, has become crazy for Him! It's amazing how God works!

An Angel Helps Me to Put Gas in My Car

One Wednesday evening, while I was driving to church with Sanjay for Bible study, the car ran out of gas only a short block away from the gas station. I usually drive with at least half a tank, but had driven the car quite a bit that week and planned to fill up on my way to church. Sanjay was only nine years of age at the time. I left him in the locked car, with the instruction not to open the door for anyone, and started to walk the hundred yards or so to the gas station, praying quietly, "Lord, I need Your help. I don't know how to put gas in the car." (I know now, thank God!)

Suddenly, a man stepped across my pathway. He was wearing a white shirt with gray trousers and was carrying a small, black leather briefcase under his arm. When I apologized and asked for his help, he smiled and walked with me to the gas station. He was so helpful, and I thanked him a few times for his kindness. During our short conversation, I told him that I was a born-again Christian and was on my way to church. He exuded such a gentle spirit that I took the liberty to ask if he was a born-again Christian. He smiled and said, "No." Curiously, and out of my normal character, I inquired what his profession was, and he told me that he was in the insurance business.

When we returned to the car, he shook Sanjay's hand and put in the gas. Thanking him again, I got into the driver's seat and slightly turned my head to pull the seat belt. When I turned back, he was absolutely gone! I said to Sanjay, "Where did he go?! Where did he go?!" I was so stunned. It was then that I realized that the Lord had heard and answered my short prayer by sending an angel to help me put gas in my car.

After I finished shouting with joy and had calmed down, the Holy Spirit gave me the interpretation of my encounter. Since God's holy angels are sinless created beings, they cannot be "born again" as Christians are. Also, according to the Holy Bible, angels are sent by God to ensure the protection of God's people and to minister to them. They are our insurance agents. Glory!

I just knew as we drove to church that this angel was sitting on the top of the car, going to church with us, and having a great time up there.

> For He shall give His angels charge over thee, to keep thee in all thy ways. (Psalm 91:11)

> Are they not all ministering spirits, sent forth to minister for them who shall be heirs of salvation? (Hebrews 1:14)

"Mom, Where's the Beef?"

Now that I was a Christian and no longer worshiped the cow, I wanted to learn how to cook ground beef and mentioned this to my son. He thought it was a good idea, so I asked my friend, Dee, about it. She was delighted to help me and explained how to cook it. Of course, I didn't know what to expect but forged ahead valiantly.

The grand day came when I announced to Sanjay that we would be eating ground beef for lunch. He was happy about that. Taking the ground beef to the kitchen sink and unwrapping the package, I washed it and washed it and washed it and washed it...not fully realizing that the pieces of ground meat were slipping through my fingers and going down the sink. I ended up with hardly any meat. Right then, my son came into the kitchen and asked, "Mom, where's the beef?" Needless to say, it was down the sink!

I telephoned Dee. "Why can't I wash the ground beef? Each time I try to wash it, it just keeps slipping through my fingers and going down the sink." My dear friend, Dee, laughed so hard that she couldn't talk. Finally composing herself, she explained to me that ground beef is not to be washed and that is why she never told me to wash it. Though it was funny and we both laughed, I thought how important it is to follow instructions.

I did try cooking ground beef after this hilarious episode. I thought it came out fine, and my son and I haltingly ate it.

Dear reader, you can never imagine what emotions I experienced while sitting at the kitchen table, staring at the meat, and shaking my head. To think that I once worshiped the cow, and now I was cooking the cow! The very idea! What a difference JESUS makes when HE opens our spiritual eyes and understanding.

The Creator, the living and true God, alone is to be worshiped. Nothing and no one else.

I must also add that I have nothing against the cow, but I know for a fact that we will never, ever, ever be good friends. I prefer vegetables, or even chicken.

My Christian Growth

My Christian growth continued as I sought the Lord with all my heart, attending every church meeting, sometimes waiting for the door of the church to be opened because I was so early. It was also a joy to serve in several ministries in the church. I was hungry for the things of God. The Lord graciously continued to teach me as I soaked myself in the Word of God. I was a dry and thirsty soul who needed the life-giving water of the Holy Spirit. Bible studies, prayer, worship, and reading and studying the Bible for myself were all major parts of my Christian walk. In spite of all my flaws, I simply loved Jesus.

Being a single parent raising a young child and working full-time, I took my son to church as often as possible so that he could grow in the ways of the Lord. When he couldn't attend church with me, I paid a babysitter to watch after him.

Photo Album

My precious Ma

Prema at 22 in Toronto

Working in the bank

Celebrating Diwali with Sanjay

Prema in Toronto

Kashmir, India

On the way to Vaishno Devi Mandir

At the Ganges River

At the Ganges River

On my way to bathe in the Ganges

At Mahatma Gandhi's tomb in New Delhi

In Sanjay's grandparents' store in India

Temple worship in Punjab

At the Golden Temple, Amritsar, Punjab

Yes, Lord God, I believe

Chapter 20
Supernatural Experiences

On one occasion, I was part of a ladies' group on a church retreat in the country. Deciding to go out alone for a walk very early in the morning, I stopped at a bridge to look at the beauty of the sun as it rose up in the sky. It was such a beautiful, golden, and bright morning. Standing there and looking at God's creative power, I wept in gratitude as I thanked my Daddy for giving me the privilege of being His child and allowing me to witness His beautiful creation with new and appreciative eyes.

Except for my own heart-felt praises to the Lord, the place was very quiet. Suddenly, I heard such a beautiful chorus of voices singing a heavenly melody. I didn't know the language they were singing in, but I knew that they were praising the Lord. I didn't see anyone, but their voices were moving back and forth, swooping up and down, and dipping in the air all around me.

Their singing brought a sacred joy and deep emotion to my heart. I was made to understand that this was a band of holy angels who were praising God for His goodness and His love.

My heavenly Father has allowed me to hear the angels sing many times, sometimes at church.

The Bible says in Psalm 113:3:

From the rising of the sun unto the going down of the same, the LORD'S Name is to be praised.

The Face of Christ in the Storm

One night, the Lord gave me this vision:

It was a dark night, and the clouds were gathering and moving very quickly. The whole place looked gray and gloomy. Suddenly, I noticed a face in the passing clouds. It was the face of Satan. It looked so ugly and angry, with his jaws squared and clenched, as if he was about to kill someone. His dark and threatening expression was one of great rage.

The clouds continued to move hurriedly as the storm gathered. In the midst of the stormy clouds, another face appeared. It was that of my Lord Jesus. He was smiling broadly at me with a calm and serene expression, assuring me that all was well, even in the midst of the storm.

The Prince of Peace is amid the storms of life. How reassuring and comforting! Praise the Lord!

"In the Name of Jesus!"

One night, the Lord gave me this experience in a dream. I was in a farmer's field with many of God's children. Suddenly, from the sky, arrows were being shot directly at us from unseen hands. These arrows were falling all over, and as they came down, I noticed that they were of different colors. Many of God's children were struck to the ground and paralyzed by them.

As each arrow came towards me, I pointed to it and in faith declared, "In the Name of Jesus! In the Name of Jesus!" When I said this, the arrows missed me and fell by the wayside. Not one arrow from the enemy harmed me.

Thank God that His people are privileged to use the Name of our Lord Jesus, rendering the enemy of our souls helpless.

My Father Whispers, "God Is Love"

One day while in prayer, I felt the love of God in such a profound way that I started to weep and sob. I said to my Father, "Daddy, how could You love me so much?"

My Father gave me an open vision of a huge, round mound, something like a very large upside-down basin. Close to the base of this huge mound was a very tiny speck. I understood that the huge mound, symbolically, was the Lord in comparison to the tiny speck, which was me.

Then, in an audible and soft voice, my Father whispered to me, "God is Love."

He that loveth not knoweth not God; for God is love. (1 John 4:8)

Two Open Visions of the Lord Jesus Christ

Every Friday night, after making sure that my son was safely cared for, I used to spend time in prayer, waiting before the Lord, at the altar in the church with my very dear friend, Doris. We did this together for several years. Doris loved the Lord, and we always had a marvelous time in His holy presence, dancing joyfully before Him in praise and worship.

This particular night, another sister had joined us. We had been praying since 11 PM, and it was then into the early morning of the next day, Saturday, September 27, 1986. Beginning to feel cold, I got up, picked up my coat, and placed it over my shoulders.

Returning to my half-kneeling, half-sitting position on one side of the altar, I slightly glanced at my watch. It was 2:20 AM. Immediately, I noticed a shift in the atmosphere around me and started to feel a heavy, tangible presence of the Lord. I knew something was about to happen, so with my head bent in expectancy, I quietly waited before the Lord. God gracefully granted me two open visions:

I felt the crown of my head being lifted up and literally felt very hot oil being poured into my skull (not in a painful, but in a very pleasant and powerful way). The suffering Savior of the world, my wonderful Lord Jesus, then appeared to me, hanging on the Cross. He was wearing a loin cloth, and His head drooped toward His chest. As I saw this vision of my precious Savior, pain entered my soul, and hot tears stung my eyes.

Suddenly, I realized that my spirit was outside my body. My body was still half-kneeling and half-sitting, but my spirit was standing.

Regarding my spirit standing with my body half-kneeling, 1 Thessalonians 5:23 says:

And the very God of peace sanctify you wholly; and I pray God your whole spirit and soul and body be preserved blameless unto the coming of our Lord Jesus Christ.

So, the Bible says that a person is composed of spirit, soul, and body.

In a moment, the vision of my amazing Savior hanging on the Cross was taken away, and my spirit was back in my body.

Another vision followed:

The Lord Jesus Christ manifested Himself to me again, just a few feet away. This time, He was in His royal robe of splendor! He was high and lifted up, and His train filled the temple! His beautiful, flowing robe was light blue in color, and the hem of His garment was moving slightly, being blown by a gentle breeze, the wind of the Holy Spirit.

The Lord stood about two feet above the altar in front of where I was kneeling. I shyly looked at my Master's most lovely face. He gave me the most beautiful and loving smile of welcome and acceptance that I have ever seen. His two hands were fervently stretched out to me as if to say, "Come here, My child!"

And His eyes. I cannot quite describe them. They were just the most loving, caring, gentle eyes of fiery love one could ever imagine! To me, they looked blue mixed with a bit of green. The best way I can describe the Lord's eyes is to say that they were like tumbling rivers of pure love, drawing me and gently pulling me into His loving embrace. I also noticed that the Lord's hair, which reached down to His shoulders, was a beautiful light brown, as if reflected by a golden light. It was also in many beautiful curls.

As I looked into His wonderful and smiling face, I automatically covered my eyes with my hand in a shy blush. When I looked up again, my Lord Jesus was gone. I was in a state of awe. Such an anointing came over me that I felt as if I could tackle the giant Goliath and conquer him with my little finger.

I started from a whisper – to a semi-loud voice – to a shout, "I saw the Lord!!! I saw the Lord!!!" By then, my sisters were caught up with me in my joy, knowing that something very special had happened. We picked up tambourines and marched and danced around the church sanctuary, singing at the top of our voices! It was 4:30 AM.

I had spent more than two hours in the presence of my precious Lord, Master, and King. At the time, it seemed like two minutes. His smile is what I will always remember. Of all the visions that the Lord has given me, this particular imprint of my Lord's most lovely face will always stay with me in a special way.

To God be all the glory, now and forever! Thank You so very much, my precious Lord. You are so very gracious.

The Agony of the Christ Amid Thousands of Angels

The Lord gave me this dream/vision as I was sleeping:

I was in a park near my apartment, and I had gone to use the ladies' room. Someone was standing behind the door, and as I opened it, the door slightly struck her. Instead of apologizing to her, I rudely asked if she couldn't see me coming in. Immediately, I was convicted by the Lord for my bad behavior. I asked the lady to forgive me, which she did.

Walking back outside, still feeling remorseful and kicking the grass and gravel with my shoes, I looked up and noticed that the sky was a threatening, stormy black and gray. In the center of the stormy clouds was the Lord Jesus Christ nailed to the Cross. I saw Him from the side. He was still alive, and His right leg was jerking in agony. My heart hurt with extreme grief and sadness as I saw my Lord in such terrible pain.

Within a few seconds, I saw thousands of angels entwined in a huge circle in the sky all around Him. They were all looking at the Lord. Suddenly, the sky lit up, turning golden as light from the Son of God and from all the angels invaded the darkness.

Through this experience, I felt that the Lord was saying to never forget what He has done for me. He was reproving me for my behavior, but He was also saying to keep marching on for His glory. Thank God for His great mercies upon us! God is sovereign and can speak to us in so many different ways, among which are dreams and visions.

"Be Ready for the King!"

One of the first things I learned when I became a Christian is that Jesus is coming back and everyone must be ready.

This dream/vision was given to me as I slept:

I was standing by a water fountain. Suddenly, I heard a trumpet sounding with loud, long blasts. As I looked up, a very huge angel was flying through the sky, blowing through a large, golden trumpet:

"Be ready for the King! Be ready for the King!"

This announcement came out as a warning.

I prostrated myself to the ground in worship of our Lord.

While I was coming out of sleep, I found myself speaking in my heavenly language and praising the Lord.

CHAPTER 21
CALLED INTO FULL-TIME MINISTRY

Although I enjoyed my job immensely at the bank, the Lord had been stirring my heart with a deep desire to serve in full-time ministry. I know that we can serve the Lord anywhere and anytime, and I did volunteer at church in several ways, but I just wanted to get into full-time ministry work. So, for two years, I prayed at the altar with much weeping that God would open the right door for me.

One morning, during my prayer time, the Lord gave me a promise from His Word:

I will instruct thee and teach thee in the way which thou shalt go: I will guide thee with Mine eye. (Psalm 32:8)

Thank God for His Word.

One day at work, I received a telephone call from a customer asking if he and his daughter could meet with me. They were nice people, and I had witnessed to them before about Jesus and His love. "Sure," I said, not knowing what they wanted to see me about. We met at the restaurant next door for about half an hour.

Mr. K went straight to the point. "Prema," he said, "for the last year, my daughter and I have been watching you as you work. I will be retiring in a few months, and my daughter will be taking over as president of my company. I would like to offer you the position of vice-president." My mouth dropped open, and at that moment, I was so glad that I had my real teeth! If not, from what I was just offered, right then and there, my false teeth might have fallen out!

Mr. K offered me a salary that was eight thousand dollars more per year than I was earning at the bank, with a four-and-a-half day work week. They told me that they didn't need an answer right away but encouraged me to seriously consider their offer. I sat there listening, shocked beyond belief.

I kindly thanked him and told him that, as a Christian, I would have to pray about it first. He seemed bemused by my answer. Doubtless to him, the most logical thing to do would be to grab the job. It would be more pay and being a single parent, for goodness sake, what do you have to pray about?

After we parted, I asked the Lord to help me continue being a good witness for Him. Here were these dear people observing my Christian walk for a whole year, without my even noticing!

My heart was set for ministry work, but this offer seemed so practical – and tempting. Then the old enemy whispered to my mind, "Don't forget now, you are a single parent and would be making eight thousand dollars more a year, with only a four-and-a-half day work week. That would be ideal for you! Besides, you would have more time to spend with your son and more money. Now, don't be a fool and miss this opportunity!"

But, thank God for His Holy Spirit Who lives inside the believer. He reminded me of God's promise to lead and guide me, and so I started to sing! I also told the enemy what I thought of him, and in Jesus' Name where to go! Sincerely seeking the Lord for direction, I knew in my heart that the job was not for me. It was good – but it was not God's perfect will for me. Christian ministry work was what I had desired and prayed for. I sent Mr. K and his daughter a card, sincerely thanking them, but declining their kind offer.

Three months later, he telephoned me again. "Prema, the job is still available. Have you changed your mind?" I explained to him that I had prayed about it and felt the Lord was not leading me in that direction. He was gentle and understanding but mentioned that he was hoping I had reconsidered his offer. He expressed his disappointment.

My total desire is to always be in God's perfect will, and the Lord was teaching me that it usually comes with a price. Nevertheless, I continued to seek the Lord for full-time Christian work because that is what He had put in my heart. My Father was very gracious to answer my prayers.

The church which my son and I attended had a separate ministry. It was also an international distributor of Christian books, tracts, and tapes to fifty-four countries. In 1988, I was hired as a staff member of the church and, a few months later, became an international coordinator for this ministry. My pastor, who was also my employer, explained that I would be in touch with several countries on a daily basis, dealing with a variety of issues. On a given day, it was no surprise to speak to someone in Africa, China, India, France, the United States, or anywhere else in the world. I truly enjoyed my job.

A few years later, I went on to become the office manager, overseeing a mailing list of seven thousand names and addresses. I also took a pay cut of five thousand dollars, but that was okay because I was just thrilled to life that the Lord had heard and answered my prayers! God is faithful and really does work in mysterious ways, His wonders to perform. The Lord also never fails. Despite the pay cut, He always provided for my son and me.

Marriage

However, after several years, a serious situation occurred at my home church, and the Lord led me to another church, this one much smaller. Within a week, I was hired as the church secretary. One day, while I was working in the office, a Canadian brother introduced himself to me as Peter. A short time after, he asked me to marry him. When I shared this news with my son, he was very happy for me but asked the question, "Already?" Wise child! However, he and Peter got along well, and on a bright and sunny Saturday afternoon, with many family members and friends present, we were married.

My son and I had lived alone for fourteen years, and since I was no longer single, changes were inevitable. Peter would often remind me – with a smile – that the Lord had sent him to be my sandpaper. To tell the truth, in the midst of adjusting to married life, there were countless times when I wished that I had remained single. At one time, I even tried to run away from it all but didn't make it very far. Meanwhile, Peter has stayed very faithful to his "sandpaper assignment!" As for me, it's "one day at a time, sweet Jesus! Help me today, show me the way..."

"Daddy, I Am Upset with Peter"

One Saturday afternoon, Peter was late to lunch as he was engrossed in some ministry work. I was hungry, and when he did come, I gave him the silent treatment. After lunch, I went and lay on the couch. I was still upset when I fell asleep.

The Lord Jesus appeared to me and sat at the foot of the bed. Dragging myself to sit next to Him, I cupped my hand to His ear and whispered, "Daddy, I am upset with Peter. Daddy, I am upset with Peter."

His loving gaze just melted me. He spoke to me so kindly and gently and said, "Let it be an image, not a picture." At once, the Holy Spirit gave me the interpretation of my Lord's counsel. An image is usually like a stone or a rock – hard. A picture could easily be torn. Therefore, my marriage, or any marriage, should be like an image, not a picture. My all-wise Father!

CHAPTER 22
ORDINATION

In 1995, my husband and I, along with two other preachers, traveled to Florida for six weeks to share the Gospel. During that time we were introduced to Dr. Harold Vick, Founder and President of Jacksonville Theological Seminary. After being given a ministerial evaluation regarding my studies and experience, I was assessed with a Bachelor of Biblical Studies degree.

Two days later, at the First Foursquare Church of Jacksonville, also founded and pastored by Dr. Vick, I was ordained to the Gospel Ministry. Dr. Vick said he wanted to be the first person to put an offering towards our ministry and encouraged his congregation to also contribute. Peter and I were so blessed at the grace of God that we saw through His humble servant and his team. The Lord is so faithful!

If the Lord Jesus Christ can take the life of a broken, suicidal, Hindu woman and fix it by changing her heart through His powerful Name and Blood, I promise you, He can and will do the same for you. Call on the Name that is above every name – the Name of Jesus!

"PAID IN FULL"

During the Sunday morning church service, just before I was ordained, Dr. Vick asked me to share my testimony. I told my story of how this young Hindu girl had encountered the true and living God, the Lord Jesus Christ, at the age of twelve, how I had later traveled to India, going up the Himalayan Mountains and then bathing in the Ganges River, how I was miraculously saved in New York City by answering a newspaper ad, and how my telephone call had been answered by a pastor who himself was a former Hindu. As I gave my testimony, the congregation was moved and shouted praises to the Lord God of heaven for His mighty acts to the children of men!

After the ceremony, Sister Vick came down the aisle with tears streaming down her face. She removed the chain which she was wearing around her neck and, through her tears, placed it around mine. On it, there was a beautiful Cross bearing the words, "PAID IN FULL." She cried and hugged me.

To this day, I treasure this chain with its Cross and precious words. It speaks of the precious shed Blood of my Lord Jesus Christ which has washed away ALL my sins and has made me righteous in the sight of God, even as it says in His holy Word!

The next day John seeth Jesus coming unto him, and saith, Behold the Lamb of God, Which taketh away the sin of the world. (John 1:29)

A Diamond Ring

The pastors of We're For Jesus, a large church in Jacksonville, had asked me to share my testimony. The Lord had blessed the meeting, and He was greatly glorified. The next Sunday when we returned to the church, the pastor, Dr. Mary Jones, asked my husband and me to wait at the altar for her and her husband, Dr. Robert Jones.

As we four stood in the altar area, she turned to me and said, "Let me see your hands." She related that when I lifted my hands to glorify the Lord as I shared my testimony the previous Sunday, the Lord spoke to her and said, "Give My daughter the first ring you ever bought." She questioned, "The first ring? But Lord, that is my beautiful diamond ring with white gold. You can't mean that one." "Yes, that one," the Lord replied.

In obedience, the pastor took the expensive ring out of its case and slipped it on my wedding ring finger. It fit like a glove, as if it were made to order! My Father blessed me with a lovely, pear-shaped, teardrop, three-tiered ring which has thirty-two lovely diamond stones on it.

With a smile on his face, Pastor Robert told us that when his wife shared with him what the Lord had asked her to do, he encouraged her to do it. "Otherwise," he said, "you're going to have to book a flight, fly to Toronto, Canada, and try to find her!"

Before I became a Christian, I wore a lot of jewelry. My outfit would often include three gold chains, a nose ring, lots of golden bracelets on both hands, earrings, toe rings, anklets, and a large diamond ring with twenty-seven stones. At my job, they called me "Miss Fashion Plate." In my very pitiful and show-off state, whenever I had to point at something, I would use the finger with the large diamond ring to dazzle and impress others, especially the customers. My co-workers used to joke that if the bank were robbed, the thieves would forget about the vault and just rob me!

O vanity of vanities! Thank God for His deliverance!

I now understand that I wore jewels to cover up my terrible insecurities. I was a subtle show-off, and when the compliments came, it gave me a sense of satisfaction. I now believe that part of my behavior was in response to past rejection.

Soon after I came to know Jesus as my Lord and Savior, the Lord started to deal with me. I was led by the Lord to give away all my jewelry, including the diamond ring with twenty-seven stones. I had no desire to wear any of it.

FROM COWS AND COBRAS TO THE CROSS OF CHRIST

The Lord was beginning to teach me something very precious. I learned from the Word of God that security is not found in things that we possess, but rather in making Jesus Christ the Lord of our lives. When we allow God to have His rightful, total control over us, there is a peace that passes all understanding. As the Word of God says, *"But godliness with contentment is great gain."* (1 Timothy 6:6)

As a Christian, I believe that nothing is wrong with wearing jewelry in moderation. I believe it is a heart issue. So, having learned my lesson, the Lord replaced my former diamond ring with one that had thirty-two stones.

Our gracious God is a debtor to no one, and He is truly amazing.

When I wear the ring, some people have a problem with it, as it is quite noticeable. A lady, whom I had never seen in my life, once said to me, "You are only coming to a conference. Why the big ring?" A Christian brother let me know in no uncertain terms that when I am praying for the sick, I should not be wearing "that big diamond ring!"

My response? Just a smile. My thoughts? The Bible says repeatedly that we will all give account for ourselves to the Lord. We do well to understand what we are responsible for, and to focus on that.

More Diamonds

On one of our mission trips to Trinidad, a Christian sister came to the airport to meet me just before we boarded the plane to return to Canada. I had prayed for her on the telephone but had never met her. She handed me a small gift bag and said that the Lord told her to bless me with it. I thanked her and put her little bag in my pocketbook.

During the flight, I decided to open the present. Well, lo

and behold, Father had sent me another beautiful ring, this one with fifty small diamonds arranged in the formation of a cross.

A couple of years later, the Lord told me to give this ring to a sister in Christ. I was most happy to do it, and she was most pleased to receive it. We were two happy people, just loving the Lord. No strings attached!

Another time, another beautiful ring was given to me by a close friend whom I had met on the job years earlier. She said she just wanted me to have it. That, too, I gave to someone.

Diamonds or not, God is good – all the time! Daddy, thank You for all Your love and blessings to me. You are so awesome! I love You very much for Who You Are and for all You so lovingly do. Please help me to continue to seek Your face more than to seek Your hands.

Chapter 23
Church Planting

About a month after we returned to Canada from our Florida ministry trip, while I was in prayer one afternoon, the Lord spoke to me very clearly about planting a church. Rivers of Living Water Church was planted in Toronto on November 19, 1995, and though it was a small assembly, the Lord helped us to faithfully lead His people according to His Word.

God Writes in the Sky, "Believe El"

At about 2:30 AM on Saturday, November 18, the day before our first church service, I received this vision:

In a very blue sky, I saw written in huge, white letters the words, "Believe El."

Because in Hebrew the word "El" means God, the Lord was saying to me, "Believe God for everything, including the grace you will need in every situation."

"Yes, Lord God, I believe."

A few hours later, I was in a secondhand store getting some cleaning items for the church. An old framed picture was sticking out of a large cardboard box. It was a painting of a rough sea with a huge wave striking a tall rock in the ocean. The sky was blue. Written on this framed picture in large, white letters were the words, "Yes, Lord God, I believe."

I paid two, well-spent dollars for that sign, which we hung in the church sanctuary for every service. Since we no longer pastor, the sign is now hanging in our living room at home.

Lady Pastors

I have yet to understand why some Christians have a problem with lady pastors. In case you missed it, the Bible says that God gives gifts and callings without repentance. He calls and assigns. Man confirms.

For I brought thee up out of the land of Egypt, and redeemed thee out of the house of servants; and I sent before thee Moses, Aaron, and Miriam. (Micah 6:4)

There is neither Jew nor Greek, there is neither bond nor free, there is neither male nor female: for ye are all one in Christ Jesus. (Galatians 3:28)

Dear church family, when the Lord found me, I was so messed up. My mind couldn't think straight. I was full of hatred, anger, and fear. I was full of pride, was so self-centered, and needed so much healing.

God is bigger than each one of us. He stopped me dead in my tracks and brought LIFE to me – new LIFE. He healed my mind and helped me to rise up and overcome from the ashes of my broken life.

I would suggest that we unite in one spirit and get the job done. We should be busy doing the Lord's business, instead of attacking one another. It makes me sad to think that some people believe that, because I am a woman, I cannot be used by God in the pulpit.

As you can rightly tell, I refuse to just breathe and make it into heaven. It was the Lord Who found me when I was on my way to hell, and it was God Who called me to serve Him. He gave His life for such a wretch as I when He died on the Cross!

126

Why should I refuse to serve Him in whatever calling He has upon me? God is not limited in His gifts and callings. So why do some of God's people try to limit Him?

If the devil used me when I was not saved, cannot God use me in a greater way now that I am His child? I propose that if He could use Balaam's donkey (Numbers 22:21–35), He can surely use you – and me.

When the Lord found me and called me to serve Him, that was all the approval I needed. Surely, God will not refuse someone an entrance to heaven because a lady preacher led him/her to Christ.

And all the ladies (and some men too!) say, "Amen!"

CHAPTER 24
VISITATION – A FACE-TO-FACE ENCOUNTER WITH GOD THE HOLY SPIRIT!

If you are a born-again child of God, and Jesus Christ is your Lord and Savior, then His Holy Spirit lives in you. However, as a young Christian, my understanding of the Holy Spirit was that He is a powerful influence and a great force. Although the Lord Jesus referred to the Holy Spirit as "He," for many years my heart could not grasp that the Holy Spirit is a real Person.

The Holy Spirit is not some cloud floating in the sky, and He is much more than a force – He is God. With all His attributes, the Holy Spirit is a very lovely and real Person. And to God's glory, I had the wonderful privilege of seeing this very lovely Person – God the Holy Spirit.

In the Word of God, the Holy Spirit is called by several names and titles, such as the Spirit of God, the Spirit of Christ, the Promise of the Father, the Comforting Counselor, the Spirit of Love, and many more. In the first book of the Bible, the Word of God tells us that the Holy Spirit moved before Father God spoke light into existence. Genesis 1:1–3 says:

In the beginning God created the heaven and the earth.

And the earth was without form, and void; and darkness was upon the face of the deep. And the Spirit of God moved upon the face of the waters.

And God said, Let there be light: and there was light.

My Privileged Visitation by God the Holy Ghost

The first service of Rivers of Living Water Church was held on Sunday, November 19, 1995. It was a time of great, exuberant, thankful praises and giving of glory to our great God. Several hours of high praises going up to the throne room were the order of our worship that day. Our Lord Jesus was highly exalted, and the presence of the wonderful Holy Spirit was so tangible. Our heavenly Father was totally glorified by His children. It seemed as if the rafters rang out explosive praises of God along with us! The only thing I didn't do in my exuberant worship was swing from the chandelier. When we left the church, I was a joyfully tired and very hoarse lady – from shouting the glory of Him Who alone is so worthy!

On Monday, I was still marveling at the goodness of our great God and was in a state of extreme thankfulness, just knowing that Jesus is my Lord and Savior. All day long, I sensed His amazing grace over me. I don't know how else to explain it except to say that I felt as if praises were flowing through the pores of my skin – out of my very being. I felt my Father's deep love for me in such a special way.

When you know that you have been pulled from the pit, you cannot help but be grateful!

When it was time to go to sleep, I was still so bright-eyed. I tried playing a cassette by Pastor Bob Phillips, but the tape recorder seemed to gurgle. As I was lying on the bed, I noticed the clock's large, red, digital numbers glowing in the dark. It read, "1:03 AM." It was Tuesday morning, November 21, 1995. What happened next was one of the most extraordinary experiences I have ever had.

Suddenly, the Lord put me into a very deep sleep, a trance-like state as described in the book of Acts:

And he [Peter] *became very hungry, and would have eaten: but while they made ready, he fell into a trance.* (Acts 10:10)

I saw myself sitting on our living room couch which faced the door to the balcony. Coming from the direction of the balcony was the most awesome Person. As He started to approach me, the thought was imparted to my spirit, "This is God the Holy Ghost." His head was held high, His shoulders were thrust out, and He walked with all majesty, power, and authority. The Person of the Spirit of the living Lord God was wearing a long, rugged garment which went right down to His feet and was light gray in color with tiny, white dots all over.

Because the Lord Jesus had already appeared to me several times, the first thought I had was that the Holy Spirit looks so much like the Lord Jesus. He actually looks like His twin! However, I noticed a slight difference between Them. In the visions granted to me of our Lord Jesus, His hair was down close to His shoulders. The Holy Spirit's hair was not down but was extended outward with power. Thinking about His hair afterward, it reminded me of someone sticking his finger into a live electrical outlet.

Walking about two feet behind the Spirit of the living God was an angel who was not more than four feet tall. In human terms, he looked to be about fifteen years of age, but in my heart I knew that, though he appeared to be so young, he was thousands of years old, and was very wise.

As the Almighty Holy Spirit, this very beautiful Third Person of the Godhead, strode toward me, I stood up. The lovely Holy Spirit of God stood about fifteen inches in front of me. I found myself looking into the very blue, deep, penetrating, serious, serene, and very holy eyes of God the Holy Ghost, and I felt as if I was looking right into eternity! Because of His awesome holiness, I couldn't look into His eyes for long and found myself looking down at the carpet, trembling with fearful reverence.

I could feel the eyes of the Spirit of God penetrate my very soul. As I stood before this wonderful and divine Third Person of the Godhead, I was inspired to put out both my hands, with my palms facing upwards, and quietly ask, "Would You please pray that Jesus will always keep me?" When I said this, the Holy Spirit placed both His palms on my palms. I felt the sensation of electricity surge through my entire body.

With His pure, holy, and penetrating eyes still staring into my soul, the Spirit of God began to rub my palms with His palms, one at a time. I was then looking intently at both His hands. He slowly rubbed one palm after the other in a striding kind of way. I believe the Lord Holy Spirit rubbed my palms about eight times. As He did, I was amazed to see hot oil gushing out of the middle of His palms and flowing freely over mine.

The oil overflowed my palms and went to the back of my hands. As I stood there before the Lord, I found myself rubbing my hands, with the hot oil still overflowing and dripping on the carpet, and saying these words, "These hands shall be laid on the sick and they shall recover."

In the Scriptures, our Lord Jesus said, *"they shall lay hands on the sick, and they shall recover."* (Mark 16:18)

Without saying a word, God the Holy Spirit and the angel both turned and walked back the same way they came.

My eyes opened. I was back on the bed. The first thing I noticed was the time on the clock. It read, "1:17 AM." I believe that God arranged it so that I would see the time both immediately before and after this holy experience. For fourteen unforgettable minutes, I had a face-to-face, divine encounter with the Person of God the Holy Spirit!

I sat up in bed trembling, totally overwhelmed with this profound and divine encounter. Barely able to speak, I tried to lift my elbow to nudge my sleeping husband. After many attempts, I stuttered, "I, I, I looked into the eyes of the Holy Ghost and saw eternity!"

What an experience! What a divine experience!

In the trance, I was inspired to ask the Holy Spirit, "Would You please pray that Jesus will always keep me?" Later that day, I sought the Lord for a Scripture confirming my question. He immediately led me to Romans 8:26–27:

Likewise the Spirit also helpeth our infirmities: for we know not what we should pray for as we ought: but the Spirit Himself maketh intercession for us with groanings which cannot be uttered.

And He that searcheth the hearts knoweth what is the mind of the Spirit, because He maketh intercession for the saints according to the will of God.

A couple of days later when I tried to play the cassette which had previously gurgled, it played fine. The message was timely. Pastor Bob Phillips spoke about the Holy Spirit, and the last line in his message was from John 7:38:

He that believeth on Me, as the Scripture hath said, out of his belly shall flow rivers of living water.

How awesome is our God!

Chapter 25
A Word on the Supernatural

And it shall come to pass afterward, that I will pour out My Spirit upon all flesh; and your sons and your daughters shall prophesy, your old men shall dream dreams, your young men shall see visions:

And also upon the servants and upon the handmaids in those days will I pour out My Spirit. (Joel 2:28–29)

Coming from a Hindu background, it still amazes me that so many of my dear Christian brothers and sisters don't believe in the total Word of God, the Holy Bible. It is difficult for me to understand why many question the area of the supernatural: angels, dreams, visions, trances, and the like. They wonder, "Is this real?" Or they say, "That can't be true." Beloved, the fact that you don't understand or believe a legitimate experience doesn't make it untrue. The Bible is a supernatural book. Abraham, Joshua, Daniel, Gideon, Mary, Joseph, and so many others all had angelic experiences.

Angels ministered to our Lord Jesus after He was tested in the wilderness, strengthening Him. Two angels sat in His empty – yes – empty tomb after He rose from the dead.

Revelation 5:11 says that there are at least one hundred million angels around the throne of God. As quoted earlier, Hebrews 1:14 says that angels are sent from heaven to minister on behalf of the heirs of salvation, and Psalm 91:11 says that the Lord has given His angels charge over His people.

Regarding the Holy Spirit, without Him none of us could be saved. He is the One Who overshadowed Mary so that she was able to conceive our Lord Jesus Christ. He is the One Who draws us to our Savior. We are born again through the work of the Holy Spirit. He works through the Cross of Christ, and is the sole Divine Agent on the earth for the church. He is real, He is supernatural – He is God! – and must be treated as God!

In these last days, the Lord is pouring out His Spirit, and more than ever before, supernatural works are being manifested. A major part of the body of Christ has limited itself to a narrow vision when it comes to this reality. God wants us to enjoy Him in every way. As Jesus said in Matthew 7:9, our loving Father will not give us a stone if we ask Him for bread.

It is important for us to be open to the ministries of the Holy Spirit. In John 10, Jesus said that His sheep know His voice and they follow Him, and a stranger they will not follow. As Christians who really want to follow the Lord, we should trust the Holy Spirit to lead us and to show us things we have never seen before.

We don't have to get weird about supernatural experiences. 1 John 4:1 and 1 Timothy 4:1 warn us to test the spirits, as many false, deceiving spirits have gone out into the world. However, I believe that if we are God-fearing, God-honoring Christians, the Lord will lead and guide us, and protect us from these false spirits. We will discern truth from falsehood.

While it is important that we do not get off track, we must, at the same time, be open to the reality of what God says in His Word.

Some people have a difficult time accepting my experiences. A few years after my divine encounter with God the Holy Ghost, Peter and I were visiting a bible college. We sat in the office of a professor whom we knew, and as I shared my experience, I felt heat in my hands. I showed him my raised fingertips, a manifestation which has occurred since my Holy Spirit visitation. (See "Fire Blisters" in the next chapter.)

He listened, pulled his glasses down to the tip of his nose, put his finger to his head, and said, "It's all in your head." Well, knowing that is not so at all, I said, "No, it is not all in my head," and sweetly sang the chorus, "He is all over me and I'm bubbling up inside, bubbling up inside, bubbling up inside...!"

The Holy Spirit can manifest Himself to whomever He pleases. The Lord does not require our approval to do what He chooses to do. He is the Sovereign God, and He acts according to His infinite wisdom and righteousness. That is good enough for me.

People have asked me how I know that I saw God the Holy Spirit. Some say that the Holy Spirit cannot be seen because He is a Spirit. Yes, He is a Spirit, but He is also a Person. Whether or not we believe in heaven or hell, they still exist. Furthermore, in my first visitation of our Lord Jesus when I was only a twelve-year-old Hindu child, the thought was imparted to my heart, "This is Jesus," even though I did not know Him.

Many years ago, I met Sister Gwen Shaw and her husband, Papa Jim. They were mightily used by the Lord to encourage the body of Christ and were holding a convention in Toronto. I had previously shared my Holy Spirit experience with her on the telephone, and Sister Gwen said she was blessed hearing my story.

She later gave some real insight into my experience as she shared it with a group of pastors who were present. As Sister Gwen so rightly and wisely pointed out, "The Lord is quite able to remove the veil from the natural eyes and allow whomever He chooses to look into the things of the spirit world. He is sovereign. In heaven, the saints are all in spirit form, yet they are readily seen and recognized by one another."

1 Corinthians 12:11 says that the Holy Spirit gives gifts according to His will. God is a purposeful creator, and He does nothing without a reason. There is a reason for the anointing. God wants people everywhere to be saved, healed, and delivered. Isaiah 10:27 says that the anointing destroys the yoke of bondage. Through the working of His gifts, our Lord is glorified.

Sadly, many leaders refuse to acknowledge that the Holy Spirit is still very much active in the church. Jesus still saves by the power of His Spirit, still heals by the power of His Spirit, and still delivers by the power of His Spirit. The gifts of the Holy Spirit are still in operation today.

The Holy Spirit of the living God is not given His rightful place in the Lord's church, and this has caused the body of Christ to walk with a serious spiritual limp. Mere men have taken over and believe that they are in charge, and therefore God's people are not walking in the power of the Holy Spirit. Many of God's people are just pew-warmers when they should be devil-chasers!

For you dear leaders in the body of Christ who believe and teach contrary to what the Word of God says, beloved, you are guilty of depriving God's people of the blessings that He wants them to have. God has given gifts to His people to be used for His glory.

The question is: What are you going to say to the Lord when you stand before Him, knowing that you were responsible for such deeds? I believe that God's ministers should forget about what our denominations say, and instead should check the Bible to see what God says. It is He to Whom we will answer on that great day. With all due respect, we don't need to blindly swallow man-made doctrines in order to please others. I believe you will agree with me that if we love Him "more than these," we must faithfully feed His sheep, as we see in John 21:15–17.

Personally, I cannot tell you why the Lord has allowed me to have these experiences, except that it must be His sovereign will. All I do know is that Father is my very breath and strength, and without Him I am totally lost and undone. I love my Lord with all my life, my heart, my soul, my mind, my strength, and my understanding, and I'm so very thankful that He first loved me. In spite of my many flaws, my God means everything to me, and with His help, I want to bring Him glory and honor all the days of my life.

CHAPTER 26
THE JOURNEY CONTINUES

To the glory of the Almighty God, since that wonderful visitation by the Holy Ghost, many have been healed, and other supernatural manifestations have occurred.

Fire Blisters

Often, I can feel my hands and my feet burning with the anointing of the Holy Spirit. My fingertips will become visibly raised up, even looking swollen. This happens especially when I speak about our Lord Jesus Christ and the anointing of the Holy Spirit. Our church members called them "fire blisters" because that is how they look.

When I asked my Lord what this means, He laid upon my heart that He has left His mark on my hands. He has blessed my hands with a tangible healing anointing for Jesus' glory and the extension of His kingdom.

When God anoints a vessel, it is for service. It is by His grace, and there is a reason for the anointing.

The Holy Shadow of Almighty God, My Lord

He that dwelleth in the secret place of the Most High shall abide under the shadow of the Almighty. (Psalm 91:1)

During my time of fellowship and prayer with the Lord, the shadow of the Lord's gentle presence falls over me, whether my eyes are open or closed, whether it is daytime or nighttime. As soon as I kneel and whisper, "My Lord Jesus," or "Daddy," or "My Sweet Holy Spirit," something wonderful happens. The Holy Spirit comes like a gentle swoosh. When the Lord's shadow falls, I feel wrapped up in His arms. Sometimes, my body vibrates with His touch. At times, I awake from sleep, shaking with the anointing and the divine touch of the Holy Ghost. He is awesome!

The Hand of the Master

During my prayer time, I often feel the slight pressure of the Lord's hand being placed on my right shoulder. It is a touch of such gentleness and comfort, coming from the wonderful Holy Spirit. Sometimes He gently embraces me. My Lord is real, and I love Him so!

Our Lord longs for fellowship, and He is always waiting for us to meet with Him. Sometimes we get so busy and keep Him waiting and waiting, and before we know it, the day is over. I have done that so many times, and yet the Lord is so patient with me. He truly is a good Father and deserves all our adoration and praise.

Quiet times of fellowship with the living and true God – just being in His presence – is truly vital to our Christian walk. Spending time with the Master, which can include telling Him how wonderful He is and how much we appreciate Him and His great salvation, is well pleasing to Him. The price He paid was so great that we must never forget that He first loved us, washing us in His very own Blood! What a wonderful Savior!

God is so good, and if we want to draw closer to Him, we must make the wise choice of putting aside the temporal feelings of the flesh and meet with Him in the secret place. Sometimes during the night, when my whole body vibrates as the Holy Spirit awakens me, the flesh wants to just sleep or stay under that warm blanket. I will start praying in my heavenly language and before you know it, I am fast asleep! Oh, how convicted I feel when I awake. Thank God for the Holy Spirit Who helps us to repent when we just want to pamper the flesh.

Awakened by the Breath of the Holy Spirit

In the early hours of the morning, I am often awakened by the Holy Breath of the Spirit of the living God. The Holy Spirit blows or breathes into my ear, usually my left ear. He simply wants fellowship.

It says in Isaiah 50:4:

The Lord GOD hath given me the tongue of the learned, that I should know how to speak a word in season to him that is weary: He wakeneth morning by morning, He wakeneth mine ear to hear as the learned.

There are times when the sweet Holy Spirit gives me bright eyes even though I have had only a couple of hours of sleep.

Shafts of Lightning

Very often, I see the light of the Holy Spirit around me, like shafts of lightning from God's throne. I used to think that someone had turned on a light behind me. The light is sometimes white or gold in color, and it seems to be layered. I give praise to my God.

The Golden Oil of the Holy Spirit

One Saturday afternoon, while sitting at my desk preparing Sunday's sermon, something very unusual happened. Right in the middle of my studying, I felt something moving on the top of my head.

At that time, mad cow disease was prominent in the news and people were getting sick and even dying from it. The news mentioned that this disease attacks the body and causes problems with the head.

For the life of me, I couldn't understand what was happening. I didn't know what to think or who to talk to. I don't quite like hamburgers, but maybe once or twice a year, I would get one. My mind was beginning to wonder and think back, "Now, Prema, the last time you ate a hamburger, gulp, was at least two months ago..."

I was concerned and prayed about what was happening to my head. Instead of waiting for the Lord to answer, I got on the telephone. The three people I spoke to didn't have a clue what I was talking about. Two of them had been in the ministry for over forty years and said they had never heard of such a thing.

At this point, the enemy of my soul was trying to put fear in my heart, and whispered, "You have mad cow disease. Why do you think you are too special to get it? Everyone is getting it. You too." Imagine the audacity of the father and creator of lies! That creep was waiting to inch right in. "In Jesus' Name," I loudly rebuked that strange voice and once more called on the Name of my Lord.

Slumping to my knees, I was determined to hear from the Lord. I desperately needed an answer. That is what I should have done in the first place. Sometimes we run to people, when in fact we should be running to the Lord. People do not have all the answers all the time, but God does! Amen.

Whatever was moving on my head was still moving. I needed an answer.

Well, bless His most holy Name, as I continued to pray and seek the Lord that afternoon for an answer to this strange occurrence, another amazing thing began to happen. Starting from the top of my head and flowing all over was the physical sensation of oil. It felt as if hot oil was being poured all over my head!

Dearly beloved, from that day until now, this outpouring of the golden oil of the Holy Spirit has never stopped. Sometimes, I feel it to a greater extent than at other times, but it is a daily outpouring and anointing of the oil of the Holy Spirit. As this happens, I literally feel the weight of the Lord's glory. It is His blessed and most wonderful Holy Presence. I don't know how else to describe it, except to say that when the Lord God pours His oil on my head, it feels as if I am wearing a heavy and tightly-fitted crown. Praise God! Jesus is Lord!

Thou preparest a table before me in the presence of mine enemies: Thou anointest my head with oil; my cup runneth over. (Psalm 23:5)

I have found David My servant; with My holy oil have I anointed him. (Psalm 89:20)

The Rain and Dew of the Holy Spirit

For I will pour water upon him that is thirsty, and floods upon the dry ground: I will pour My Spirit upon thy seed, and My blessing upon thine offspring. (Isaiah 44:3)

The first time the rain of the Spirit fell over me, I was expounding the Holy Scriptures while visiting a church. As soon as I opened my mouth to speak, I felt as if rain was falling over me.

Several months later, while on my knees in prayer at church before Sunday morning service, it happened again. It was a cold November day, and I was wearing a thick sweater. Suddenly, I felt a huge, cold raindrop penetrate my sweater and touch my arm. We were renting a building to hold services, so my first reaction was to look up. I wondered if there was a broken pipeline somewhere but couldn't see anything.

After prayer, I shared my experience with the congregation and as I did, it seemed as if buckets of water were being poured over me. It was no longer a drop but a flood. For the Lord's glory, I sometimes still experience this.

Spiritual Mantles

Many times, a spiritual mantle is thrown over my shoulders. It is as if someone is standing behind me and placing, draping, or throwing a cloak over me. When that happens, there is an increase in the anointing as I pray for people.

Here is just one example: We were in the middle of a church service on a Sunday morning, when the mantle was draped over my shoulders. I walked down to the altar area to pray for a visitor. Standing before him, I began to feel great physical pain through my body. Having experienced this sensation at other times, I said to this man, "Son, I don't know you, but the Lord shows me that you are in deep pain." "Yes," he sobbed, "my wife was burnt to death two weeks ago." Thank God, that morning he received the Lord Jesus Christ into his heart.

Sparkles on My Hands

One Sunday morning at church, as I opened my Bible after worship to begin reading the Word of God, I went into shouting a "Hallelujah Chorus!" Both the front and back of my hands were covered with beautiful, sparkling gold dust. I became so excited that I called for God's people to quickly come forward and see this for themselves. To God be all the glory!

We know that we must be very careful, especially in these end times. We need to ask God to help us discern truth from error as we try the spirits. However, at the same time, God is on the move, and He is doing new things in His church.

CHAPTER 27
MY FAMILY'S REACTION TO MY CONVERSION

A year after I became a born-again Christian and child of the living and true God, I went back to Trinidad for a visit. My family was in great shock and needless to say, they were very disappointed with me. As expected, I was received with much ridicule and was asked, "Who exactly do you think you are? You left here as a Hindu and are coming back to tell us that this Jesus Christ is the only way to God? Who are you? Who is this new God? You are making us shame."

As they told me during my visit, and in no uncertain terms, "In all our generations, we stayed faithful to the Hindu religion. We were born into Hinduism. We are Hindus. What is this new thing? Prem, why did you do this to us?" The air was thick with resentment, along with name calling, and the enemy was trying to taunt my mind.

As I was growing up, I was so loved and accepted. Now, I was considered to be a curse to my family. I was termed a traitor to my race. I was scornfully accused of taking "the white man's God." I was insultingly ridiculed for leaving my religion. Because I was accused of bringing this strange religion of Christianity into our household, my people saw me as a great troublemaker and told me so. I felt like a total outcast. This hurt me so much, because these were the people who had loved me dearly and took great care of me. I loved them dearly too, but I had made a commitment to follow the living and true God, and I had to keep my promise to the Lord.

My Ma

Even my beloved and precious Ma was so angry with me. She was pained and truly troubled. I was very close and dear to her heart, as she was to mine, and so it broke my heart to see Ma hurt. She scolded me very much and sometimes would not speak to me. This was unlike the Ma I knew and loved. It was almost unbearable, and I felt torn inside, but God had opened my eyes to truth, and all I could do was pray for my lovely people who were lost without Christ.

One time, before Ma went to do special temple prayers, I had asked her not to offer me any of the special edible offering (prasad) upon her return, as I couldn't and wouldn't accept it. My Ma was very hurt. The prasad is the holiest part of the offering. It is first offered up to the Hindu gods, and for someone to refuse to partake of it is highly insulting. With her well-meaning and kind heart, my Ma still offered it to me, and again I had to gently tell her that I was sorry for hurting her, but I was unable to accept it. My family thought I had gone mad. Refusing the prasad was considered to be the final, total proof of my complete insanity!

It made matters worse for me when our Hindu pundit complained to Ma that he had "received a letter and some Christian papers in the mail from Prema." I had mailed him some Gospel tracts along with a letter about my conversion. Ma said she felt as if she were going to faint when he told her what I had done. She said, "Prem, you already did such a hurtful thing and put us all to shame. Did you have to also write the pundit?" She was obviously very upset about it.

I explained to Ma that I had sent him that information because Jesus loves him, and he, too, needed to know Jesus, just as everybody else does. If he were to come to know Jesus, then he could tell others about the true way to God, as God doesn't want anyone to perish. I told my Ma that even though he had been the Sankar family's pundit for all those years, he still needed Jesus in his life. She was speechless with consternation. She didn't know what to say to me, what to do with me, or what to do about me! Again, she looked at me as if I were a mad woman who needed to be locked up forever – and very soon at that.

Building Up the Temple of the Lord

During my month-long visit, Uncle Sone's children would gather around me, and I would try to quietly teach them a few short choruses that I had learned at church. Their favorite one was:

"Building up the temple, building up the temple,
Building up the temple of the Lord.
Boys, won't you help us? Girls, won't you help us?
Building up the temple of the Lord."

I was unaware that, while we sang, my Pa was keenly listening. As we sang one day, my dear grandfather peered his head through a window and sternly commented, "Yes, teach them to build up the temple of the Lord. The one we have in the yard is not good enough!" He slammed the window shut. We kept building up the temple of the Lord – just very quietly.

The seeds that were planted by Auntie Ruth in my own heart when I was a child had taken root. Without my understanding it, these seeds were also taking root. I was told that the children continued to sing that chorus long after I returned to Canada.

My Dear Mother

As for my dear mother, she also thought I had fallen overboard. She once said to me, "You were born a goat, and now

149

you are telling me that you are a sheep?" I calmly replied, "My Father is the Shepherd." She would tell people, "Prem goes to church eight days out of seven." Eventually, my dear mother stopped communicating with me altogether. This went on for several years.

One night, I was in her neighborhood and knocked on her door, hoping to at least see her. When my mom saw me, she refused to let me in, literally pushing me away as I tried to enter. "As far as I am concerned, you are dead!" she finally said, slamming the door shut. I stood there for a moment, quite heartbroken, not knowing what to do. During the forty-five minute drive home, I shed many tears and kept praying for my mother's salvation. All my letters to her were returned, marked "Refused by addressee."

All I could do was stand on the promises of God and trust the Lord to intervene. I wept much for my mother's soul, but God gave me peace, and I felt confident that my Lord would show Himself faithful to me. I had to believe! I had no other family member close by to turn to for comfort or for prayer. Since my family had turned their back on me, as much as I loved them all, I had to walk without them and without their love. My Lord Jesus Christ was worth my pain, my sadness, my loneliness, and my life. Yes, it was a very painful time. However, in the Bible the Lord promises that *He* will never leave us nor forsake us, and He never has!

Throughout this time, one of the greatest crosses I had to bear was learning that my own mother had reported me to the Children's Aid Society. I was so disheartened and became discouraged. The report alleged that I had joined a cult and was so busy with them that I was neglecting my son. If the CAS believed that, then I could end up losing my son – my only child! I took it to the Lord in prayer and asked a couple of others to pray as well.

When the social worker came home to talk to me, she saw that Sanjay was a well-balanced, happy, bright, and stable child. After perceiving that there was no truth to the report, she was intrigued listening to my testimony. In the end, she was able to spend more time listening to my conversion story than having to investigate the charges! Preparing to leave, she told me that she was encouraged. God has a fine way of vindicating His people. As He says in His Word, He will fight for us as we hold our peace. God is so good!

Dear reader, the members of my family have always been very good people, but they just didn't understand that I had been touched by the living and true God. They saw the change in me, yet they fought me tooth and nail. I was the laughingstock of my family, and as far as they were concerned, I was crazy for converting to another faith.

It broke my heart to see my family's reaction. These were people who loved me, and whom I loved, yet they were like strangers to me. However, I knew that for me, there was no turning back. As the song says,

"I have decided to follow Jesus,
I have decided to follow Jesus,
I have decided to follow Jesus,
No turning back, no turning back.

Though none go with me, I still will follow,
Though none go with me, I still will follow,
Though none go with me, I still will follow,
No turning back, no turning back.

The world behind me, the Cross before me,
The world behind me, the Cross before me,
The world behind me, the Cross before me,
No turning back, no turning back."

151

This Christian hymn originated in India.

As I started to grow in my newfound faith, reading the Bible, praying, fasting, and participating in church fellowship all became important components of what I had discovered to be a whole new way of life.

I knew that God would continue to give me the grace and strength that I needed to keep following Him. There would be no turning back.

CHAPTER 28

WHAT HAS HAPPENED TO MY FAMILY SINCE MY CONVERSION

For He is faithful that promised. (Hebrews 10:23)

My Aunt from New York

A year after I became a Christian, my aunt from New York, who swore that she was born a Hindu and would die a Hindu, walked into a church and gave her heart to the Lord Jesus Christ. Despite several personal, challenging issues, my aunt continues on her journey with the Lord. Thank You, Jesus!

My Uncle Sonerchan

My Uncle Sonerchan, whose name means gold and silver in English, is truly a precious gem of a uncle. Two years younger than I, and known as "Sone" to everyone, it had long been decided among the elder members of the family that he would be the next one to take charge of the temple after Ma passed on.

When Uncle Sone found out that I had become a Christian, he was livid with rage. In the presence of several of his friends, he beat his chest with his fist and called me a few names that I have since long forgotten. Without understanding anything about Christianity, whenever our paths crossed, he would sarcastically announce, "Here comes the pope!" God graced me with a forehead of steel to endure the insults and not retaliate. I kept praying for my precious family.

Within about two years, his wife became extremely ill and awoke every morning with bites and bleeding scratch marks on her hands and neck. She went down to a skeletal frame, and no Hindu pundits or pujas were able to help her. My uncle lost all his livelihood trying to find a cure for his dear wife.

Upon learning of her condition, I decided to visit him, even at the risk of being thrown out. I went to his house and once more talked about the saving power of my Lord and Savior Jesus Christ, Who, I added, is also able to heal anyone. This time, he paid attention to what I said and then gave me permission to lay hands and pray over both of them.

With my heart bursting with joy, I prayed for their salvation and healing, claiming them both for the kingdom of the living God. Still being very suspicious and careful of my new religion, Uncle Sone wasn't ready to go any further with the Lord. However, I was thrilled to see his progress and understood that it was God, and God alone, Who was mightily at work!

It was shortly after returning to Canada that I received a letter from my beloved Uncle Sone. "Dear Prem, you will be happy to know that Aunt Sylvia is feeling much better. She is eating well and has even put on some weight. We went to a Pentecostal church, and the pastor prayed over us. We have both given our lives to Jesus Christ. Jesus is real, Prem! I didn't know that. As the pastor said, 'You have to take a step of faith.' We did. This thing is real, Prem!"

The letter continued, "I must also tell you that the next time you come back home, you will notice something different. There is no more temple in the yard. I decided that, now that I am serving the living and true God, and the Bible forbids worshiping idols, images and statues, I had to get rid of the temple. I tore it down. I now go to church and want to honor the Lord Jesus Christ with my life. I realize that I cannot go to church to worship Jesus and also worship the Hindu gods in the temple at the same time. I had to make a choice."

Uncle Sone's letter had more. "One more thing. You remember how angry I was with you for changing your religion? I didn't understand at the time, but I understand now. Prem, I want to ask you to please forgive me. I am sorry for the way I treated you. I really didn't understand. I love you. Yours affectionately, your Uncle Sone."

When I read my uncle's letter, all I could do was fall on my face before my wonderful Father God, weep for hours, and worship my Lord Who alone is so faithful! I cried, danced, sang, and cried some more. I was giddy with joy! What a time of rejoicing it was for me to see how the Holy Spirit was touching my Hindu family, one member at a time. My family – who once knew only Hinduism and idol worship. My family – referred to by some as "the people with the temple on Sankar Street." Thank You, Lord Jesus!

Uncle Sone was sitting in his car when he first saw Peter. *"Upon this rock I will build My church!"* he shouted out to us as he waved. We both shouted back, *"And the gates of hell shall not prevail against it!"* (Matthew 16:18)

He shared with us, "Prem and Peter, I couldn't wait to get home that day. I knew that I had to make a choice for the future, for me and for my family. It was then or never. I drove up in front of the house, jumped over the gate, and ran for the sledgehammer." He said it took him days to clear everything out, but by the time he was finished, there was no longer a Hindu temple on the Sankar property. As he worked, he thought about how deceived he had been all his life. It was quite a sight for me to see that there was no longer a temple in our yard.

Thou shalt worship the Lord thy God, and Him only shalt thou serve. (Matthew 4:10)

Uncle Sone was correctly resolved to have no mixture in his walk with God. To live the Christian life, he had to do so

155

wholeheartedly. He saw the great miracle of his wife's complete healing and recognized that Jesus Christ is the only living and true God. He was totally finished with worshiping idols. To God's glory, my dear uncle and his wife have now been saved for over thirty years and have stayed true to the Lord.

As he and I discussed our miraculous conversion to Christianity, he kept pointing out how the devil uses religion to deceive people, and all the while they think that they are doing the right thing. According to the Holy Bible, God is not to be worshiped through the work of a person's hands. He created all things, and we are not to bring Him down to our created level. He is the Almighty Creator and deserves our reverence as such.

Jesus said in John 4:24:

God is a Spirit: and they that worship Him must worship Him in spirit and in truth.

A Revelation for Truth Seekers

You who are seeking truth, ask yourself this simple but profound question: What is the benefit, and what wisdom is there, in going to the forest, cutting down a tree, having a carpenter shape the wood into the form of a man, woman or animal, placing the object in a certain area of your home or temple, and then bowing down to this piece of wood that you carved with human hands? This object cannot speak, cannot hear, cannot smell, cannot move, cannot do anything. It is what it is – a painted piece of wood.

To my beloved Hindu family all over the world, please think about this with an open mind: How could a piece of wood, stone, metal, or anything else become God? Why would we mortals make "gods," and then bow down to them? God hates idol worship! It is a violation of the Word of God. It is sin.

The Ten Commandments begin with these words in Exodus 20:1–6:

And God spake all these words, saying,

I am the LORD thy God, Which have brought thee out of the land of Egypt, out of the house of bondage.

Thou shalt have no other gods before Me.

Thou shalt not make unto thee any graven image, or any likeness of any thing that is in heaven above, or that is in the earth beneath, or that is in the water under the earth:

Thou shalt not bow down thyself to them, nor serve them: for I the LORD thy God am a jealous God, visiting the iniquity of the fathers upon the children unto the third and fourth generation of them that hate Me;

And shewing mercy unto thousands of them that love Me, and keep My commandments.

My beloved family, I, too, was once deceived by the devil, but the living God opened my eyes and delivered me. He wants to do the same for you! I want you to know that the living and true God loves you so much. Call upon Jesus! He will hear and answer you. He is not a dead god, but He is alive. Worship Him. He created you for His glory.

My Uncle Sone also shared how, six months after his wife was completely healed, a friend from church spoke to him and said, "Brother Sankar, I know why you received your miracle, and I didn't receive mine. You destroyed your idols. I hid mine."

This is a major mistake which some people make after they become Christians. They compromise their faith. Some mix their walk, not understanding that God is holy and He expects His people to have nothing to do with the sin of this world. He has called us out of sin to live a holy life, not a compromised life.

Some of my Hindu brothers and sisters come to Jesus and yet keep all kinds of Hindu religious pictures. Beloved, this is not acceptable to God. The Bible warns, "*A little leaven leaveneth the whole lump."* (Galatians 5:9) Sin is like leaven. It quickly spreads and does so in a very subtle way. Compromising our faith is not an option.

The Bible expresses this principle very well in Joshua 24:14–16 and 23–24:

> *Now therefore fear the LORD, and serve Him in sincerity and in truth: and put away the gods which your fathers served on the other side of the flood, and in Egypt; and serve ye the LORD.*

> *And if it seem evil unto you to serve the LORD, choose you this day whom ye will serve; whether the gods which your fathers served that were on the other side of the flood, or the gods of the Amorites, in whose land ye dwell: but as for me and my house, we will serve the LORD.*

> *And the people answered and said, God forbid that we should forsake the LORD, to serve other gods;*

> *Now therefore put away, said he, the strange gods which are among you, and incline your heart unto the LORD God of Israel.*

> *And the people said unto Joshua, The LORD our God will we serve, and His voice will we obey.*

Decide. Choose this day whom you are going to serve. With the help of our God, let's bring glory to that matchless Name, the Name of Jesus.

This is what the Lord Jesus Himself said in John 10:10:

> *The thief* [meaning the devil] *cometh not, but for to steal, and to kill, and to destroy: I am come that they might have life, and that they might have it more abundantly.*

The devil is a deceiver! He brought you *religion*. Jesus Christ died and rose from the dead to allow you to have *a personal relationship with Him!* Faith in Him is the connecting factor in this equation. Give your life to Jesus, and when you die, you will spend eternity with Him in heaven. Without Jesus Christ as Lord and Savior, you will go to that horrible place called hell. The devil is there. Don't go there. Call on Jesus Christ.

The Name That Is Above Every Name

The Bible says in Philippians 2:9–11:

Wherefore God also hath highly exalted Him [Jesus], *and given Him a Name which is above every name:*

That at the Name of Jesus every knee should bow, of things in heaven, and things in earth, and things under the earth;

And that every tongue should confess that Jesus Christ is Lord, to the glory of God the Father.

I am so grateful to know that God loves all peoples, nations, and tribes, and He sent His Son, Jesus, to die for each one, so that we could all have life, now and forever. Eternal life!

The Bible says in Revelation 5:9:

And they sung a new song, saying, Thou [Jesus] *art worthy to take the book, and to open the seals thereof: for Thou wast slain, and hast redeemed us to God by Thy Blood out of every kindred, and tongue, and people, and nation.*

And again in Revelation 7:9:

After this I beheld, and, lo, a great multitude, which no man could number, of all nations, and kindreds, and people, and tongues, stood before the throne, and before the Lamb, clothed with white robes, and palms in their hands.

I greatly praise the Lord to see my Uncle Sone, the one who was chosen to be next in line to our Hindu temple, now saved by God's grace. He is a fearless witness for the Lord, unashamed to proclaim the Name of Jesus, the Name that is above every name. Though persecuted, harassed, and falsely accused by the enemies of Christ, by God's grace he continues to shine brightly for Jesus. The Lord has raised him up as a powerful and bold witness, a great soul-winner for Him, for a time such as this. Jesus is Lord, and to Him be all the glory!

CHAPTER 29
MORE CONVERSIONS!

My Precious Ma

I had to fly to Trinidad unexpectedly. My precious Ma was given a short time to live, and she was asking to see me. It was during this time that I began to notice a mellowing in her attitude towards me. I had broken her heart by my conversion to Christianity, and it had taken her a few years to come to terms with my faith in Jesus Christ. However, I knew that I still had to tread very gently.

Believing in the endless cycle of reincarnation that is central to Hinduism, my Ma, who always dearly loved me, suddenly shared her concern with me about the afterlife. We were in the kitchen when she unexpectedly said to me, "Prem, look how this life is. After we die, we will never see each other again."

My heart skipped a beat! "Oh, no, Ma, we *can* see each other again!" I exclaimed. "Ma, everyone was born into sin, even good people. You must ask Jesus to come into your heart and forgive you for everything, just as I did. Then when we die, we will meet again in heaven. Ma, you know how my life used to be. Jesus has given me a new life!"

My wonderful Ma stopped walking, looked at me searchingly, put her forefinger on her cheek, and thoughtfully asked me the most profound question of life, "Prem, who is Jesus?" At that moment, I thought I had grown wings and could fly! I just about did. I leapt to where she was standing and hugged her.

"Oh, my precious Ma, Jesus is God! He died for the whole world. He loves you very much, Ma. There is no one else who can take us to heaven. We die once, Ma, not over and over and over again. When I die, I am going to heaven, and we have to meet each other there. You must come with me, Ma. I love you so much!"

My Ma listened intently. She grew quiet. I knew that she was thinking about what she was hearing. I knew the Holy Spirit was touching her heart. And I knew that I had said enough for the time being...

Four months later, Ma became very ill. An aunt called from Trinidad to let me know that the doctors didn't think my precious Ma would live out the week. I was devastated. I prayed, and greatly interceded for my wonderful grandmother as never before, and reminded the Lord that His Word promises household salvation.

I wasn't physically present, but I can only imagine the great joy that both my aunt, who was visiting from New York, and my Uncle Sone experienced as they led their beloved mother – my grandmother, my precious Ma – to the Lord!

My dear Uncle Sone told me that, as he stood near Ma's hospital bed that last day of her life, he prayed to our heavenly Father, "Dear Father, please, just one more touch. Just one more touch, Father. In Jesus' Name. Amen." Along with all the other prayers, that short, heart-wrenching prayer was heard by our heavenly Father. My wonderful Ma accepted our Lord and Savior, Jesus Christ, on her deathbed.

Ma was a beautiful soul, an exceptional human being, who touched many lives in her loving and gentle way. I was told that there were at least eight hundred cars in her funeral. My

Ma is now safe in the arms of God Almighty! No more idol worshiping for her. No more Hindu temple and no more food offered up to idols. Now, she is in the presence of the living and true God, and she fully understands why Jesus died – to save a lost world, which includes every one of us. She also now fully understands why I accepted Jesus Christ as my Lord and Savior. It is by God's grace that I will meet my precious Ma in heaven, never to be separated from her again.

A few years ago, I was in a church in Toronto sharing my testimony of how the Lord Jesus has touched my life. When I shared how the Lord saved my precious Ma, the Spirit of the Lord fell upon a young lady. She shouted, cried, got up, and danced around the sanctuary!

Ma once shared with me that, many years earlier, she had a vision at a time when she was very ill and was not expected to recover.

In it, she was walking along a road in a very peaceful place that was filled with green grass and beautiful flowers. Far ahead of her, there was a man walking with a staff. Twice, she ran to try to catch up with him, but couldn't. The third time, the man stopped walking and turned around. He told her that it was not her time yet, and that she had to return. The place was so beautiful and peaceful that she didn't want to.

After Ma passed away, one of my aunts cried for a year in constant grief. One night, she dreamt that she was on a bus when she saw Ma get on. Walking directly to her, Ma asked her to stop crying, that she was in a very beautiful place filled with flowers, and that she was happy and peaceful. Upon awakening, the grief that my aunt felt was lifted from her heart.

How Great Thou Art, O Lord! How Very Great Thou Art!

My Dear Mother

My mother had never met Peter. Somehow, she found out that we were pastors at Rivers of Living Water Church. Every Sunday morning, we would come to church a couple of hours early to pray. This particular morning in December, 1996, I had gone down to the basement for something when Peter called out to me, "Someone's here to see you."

I had barely entered the sanctuary when I had the surprise of my life! There was my dear mother, loudly sobbing and running towards me, saying, "I want what you have! I want what you have!"

Oh, the joy of seeing the faithfulness of God as He moves by His mighty power!

My precious mom and I hugged and cried for a good while before I introduced her to Peter. She was overjoyed to meet him.

That morning, the God of heaven, Whose I am and Whom I serve, gave me the awesome privilege of leading my mother to Him.

As it says in Acts 3:6:

Silver and gold have I none; but such as I have give I thee: In the Name of Jesus Christ of Nazareth...

After that Sunday, it was a most amazing sight to see my mother come to church and sit at the back, watching as her daughter ministered. She had just returned from a trip to India, and though she didn't say so, I knew that she also had been searching for truth and fulfillment. "Prem, I can't believe that this is the same you!" she exclaimed. I told her that it was not my doing, but the Lord Jesus had touched me and changed my life. I told her that Jesus is able to take us out of the pit of brokenness and despair and help us to do something with our lives that will bring Him glory. We just have to allow Him to help us in our pitiful state.

My mom once said that just watching me passionately worship the Lord Jesus made her physically tired. She asked, "Where do you get the energy to worship like that?" I replied, "From the Lord." I would also sing hymns to her over the telephone, which she really enjoyed. We began to cultivate a closeness which we never had before. She asked me to forgive her for everything in the past. I told her that I had already done so, and also asked her to forgive me for anything I had ever done to hurt her.

One day when I came home from doing errands, there was an urgent message for me to call the hospital. The nurse informed me that my mother had just passed away. She had felt ill, and died within twenty minutes. I was in a daze and could hardly believe it. My dear mom and I had spoken on the telephone just two days before. The last words my precious mother said to me were, "Prem, I love you." "I love you too, mom," I had whispered back.

Our gracious Lord called my mother home only five months after she received Jesus as her Lord and Savior. She was ready to meet her Creator face-to-face.

I thought about how many times my mom had slammed the telephone down on me because she was so angry with my Christian stand. I explained to her that, though I loved her, one day each person on the face of the earth has to give account to the Lord for his or her own life. I told her that I would not be able to get by with an excuse, such as, "My mother ordered me to stop being a Christian." By God's mercy, my mom made it into heaven.

How grateful I am to the almighty and amazing God for continuing to give me the grace to stand for His glory. I have learned that pleasing God is all that really matters. I give my

Lord thanks, praise, honor, and glory for saving yet another precious soul in my family. Hallelujah! Our God is truly a great and faithful God.

So, my friends, don't give up on those hard cases that seem as if they will never receive salvation. Continue to press in and pray, believing that our God is well able to save to the uttermost. God will do His part as we do ours, no matter how difficult the situation may be. He works through His Spirit, His wonders to perform.

As I always say, being who I was, if God could save me, He can surely save anyone.

My Uncle Boyan

My Uncle Boyan was the youngest of my grandparents' children and was born a few years after me. He also was very angry with me for converting to Christianity. Whenever I tried to contact him, he would hang up the telephone. It was twelve long years before he would speak to me.

My uncle lived in Canada for five years. He had tried to get visas for his family to join him, but was unsuccessful. Having injured his back at work, he was on pain medication, which included sleeping pills. After so many years, I saw my uncle just two days before he returned to Trinidad. I told him how much I loved and missed him, and he just quietly listened. I also told him that I was still a Christian, and how much Jesus loves him. Again, he quietly listened. Then he mentioned to me how happy he was that he would be seeing his family after being away for so long.

I gave him a small gift, along with a letter which I asked him to kindly not open until he was on the airplane. In it, I told him how much he meant to me. I also explained a little about the love of God and the plan of salvation, enclosing some Gospel tracts.

He telephoned me on the morning before he left, with a confession. Unable to restrain himself, he had read my letter along with the Gospel tracts, and he thanked me very much for my letter which obviously had touched his heart.

The next I heard was that my Uncle Boyan had safely arrived in Trinidad, but was in a coma. He had encountered a very difficult situation with his family, and having no emotional or moral support, he became distraught and swallowed some sleeping pills.

When Sone (his brother) called to inform me what had happened, we cried out to the Lord for great mercy for our beloved Boyan. We prayed that the Lord would give him an opportunity to receive Christ. It felt so good to have one of my own family members praying with me through this very difficult time.

A couple of days later, as Sone was sitting at Boyan's bedside in the intensive care unit, he came out of the coma. He opened his eyes and spoke softly. Grateful for such a miraculous answer to prayer, Sone then again shared the Gospel with him.

With what little strength he had, my Uncle Boyan accepted Christ and made a commitment that, when he got better, he would serve the Lord.

A few days later, my precious Uncle Boyan slipped back into a coma and died. He was only thirty-seven years old. In my Father's great mercy, He heard and answered the cries of our hearts and gave him a chance to repent. How I praise the Lord that my Uncle Boyan made it into the kingdom of God! To God be all the glory!

Oh that men would praise the LORD for His goodness, and for His wonderful works to the children of men! (Psalm 107:8)

CHAPTER 30
MY UNCLE JAG AND MY GURU UNCLE

As I was growing up, my aunts and uncles were all so good to me. The Lord even seemed to put an extra special love for me in my Uncle Jag's heart. When I passed my Common Entrance examination at the age of eleven, he bought me a bicycle as a gift. I was so excited but didn't know how to ride it, so he taught me.

In Hindu custom, it is forbidden for girls to climb trees. However, when I was about nine or ten years old, I really wanted to pick some ripe pomeracs which were high up on this tall fruit tree. Taking a survey of my surroundings and concluding that I stood a chance, I was able to climb the tree with some difficulty as I aimed for a cluster of the fruit. Suddenly, as the wind started to blow, the branches swayed, and so did I. I was scared.

I was even more scared when a pomerac fell on the head of my Uncle Jag who was walking by! He looked up and calmly motioned with his finger for me to come down. I was let off with a strict warning to "never do that again, or else you could fall and get hurt." My wonderful uncle always made sure that I was okay. He loved me as only an older and affectionate uncle can.

Uncle Jag was a corporal in the police force. One day, he came in from work very tired and went to sleep for a couple of hours before going back for his next shift. Meanwhile, our family had made some popcorn. As a child, I was excited to share it with him, so I went upstairs and knocked on his door. Coming out of a deep sleep, he asked who it was. I said it was me and told him I had brought him some popcorn. My kind uncle didn't scold me. He lovingly took the popcorn and told me that he was going to eat it later as he needed to sleep.

At some point, Uncle Jag became a Christian, but then stopped serving the Lord.

When I learned through my family that he had become seriously ill, I would call and pray with him on the telephone, just trying to encourage him. At one time, he shared with me that he felt the Lord couldn't possibly forgive him for all the wrong things that he had done. I was happy to let my beloved uncle know that God was waiting for him to confess his sins and sincerely repent, so that he could receive forgiveness from Jesus. He was very remorseful about his past and was happy to return to our Savior, which he humbly did.

His wife had also become a Christian and was always praying for him. God answered our prayers. Thank You, Father God! You are so real.

My precious and beloved Uncle Jag died on his birthday. He was my Ma's third son.

Sometimes I picture those in my family who are in heaven now, just worshiping at the feet of the living and true God, thanking Him for the price that was paid for such great salvation. How good is the Lord!

My Guru Uncle

This uncle, whom I wrote about earlier in the book, was Ma's second son.

After I was converted to Christianity, I visited my uncle to respectfully share the Gospel with him. He listened and then said to me, "Come, child, let me show you something." We walked to his kitchen and there, on the tiled kitchen counter, was a large picture of his guru, a very well-known spiritual leader of India who died in 2011. The picture was surrounded by several garlands of flowers and lit diyas. "This is my god. This is my god." my uncle repeated.

I am sorry to say, but my uncle was a very religious Hindu who didn't receive the truth.

Jesus saith unto him, I am the way, the truth, and the life: no man cometh unto the Father, but by Me. (John 14:6)

I explained to my dear uncle about the difference between having a religion and having a personal relationship with God through Jesus Christ. He wasn't receptive to "my version of religion" and insisted that he was constantly in his temple doing his Hindu prayers, morning, noon and night.

Every one of us is born into sin through the sin of Adam, the first man created by God. The Lord Jesus was born without sin through the work of the Holy Spirit and lived a sinless life.

He, an innocent man, was crucified on the Cross of Calvary. Through the sacrifice of His life, He gave His Blood to save all people from their sins.

And they sung a new song, saying, Thou art worthy to take the book, and to open the seals thereof: for Thou wast slain, and hast redeemed us to God by Thy Blood out of every kindred, and tongue, and people, and nation. (Revelation 5:9)

Our part is to receive the Lord Jesus Christ as our personal Lord and Savior.

He was in the world, and the world was made by Him, and the world knew Him not.

He came unto His own, and His own received Him not.

But as many as received Him, to them gave He power to become the sons of God, even to them that believe on His Name:

Which were born, not of blood, nor of the will of the flesh, nor of the will of man, but of God. (John 1:10–13)

This gift, the forgiveness of our sins and resulting eternal life, is offered to us by God, but we must receive it.

We do so by humbling ourselves before God. We receive Jesus as the Lord, which means the ruler, of our life. We confess our sin and repent, which means we turn away from it. We then receive forgiveness of our sin through the Blood of Jesus that was shed on Calvary for us. Our sin is a debt that we owe to God, but Jesus paid that sin debt in full for us, that we may be set free from it. Glory to His Holy Name!

What fruit had ye then in those things whereof ye are now ashamed? for the end of those things is death.

But now being made free from sin, and become servants to God, ye have your fruit unto holiness, and the end everlasting life.

For the wages of sin is death; but the gift of God is eternal life through Jesus Christ our Lord. (Romans 6:21–23)

The forgiveness of our sin, whereby we are saved and have eternal life, is a gift which is offered to us by God. We cannot earn it by our good works or through any merit of our own.

The penalty of sin is death, eternal death. However, Jesus paid that penalty for us by dying in our place, so that we can have eternal life.

We all have a choice to make. We can choose to humble ourselves before God, and repent of our sin. We can receive Jesus as the ruler of our life, and receive that great gift which He offers us, which is the forgiveness of our sins and resulting eternal life. In short, we can choose heaven.

Or, we can refuse to humble ourselves before God, and we can refuse to submit ourselves to the One Whom He has anointed to rule over us. "Jesus" is a Hebrew name which means "The Lord is salvation." "Christ" means "The Anointed One." When we submit ourselves to the One Anointed to rule over us, we experience the salvation of God. We are saved from our sins, and have eternal life.

However, if we rebel and refuse, then we will have to pay the full consequences of our sin. We will be cut off from God for all eternity, because we rejected Jesus. We rejected His offer to rule over us in justice and righteousness, and we rejected His offer to pay the terrible price of our sin. In short, we choose hell.

Come now, and let us reason together, saith the LORD: though your sins be as scarlet, they shall be as white as snow; though they be red like crimson, they shall be as wool.

If ye be willing and obedient, ye shall eat the good of the land:

But if ye refuse and rebel, ye shall be devoured with the sword: for the mouth of the LORD hath spoken it. (Isaiah 1:18–20)

I call heaven and earth to record this day against you, that I have set before you life and death, blessing and cursing: therefore choose life, that both thou and thy seed may live. (Deuteronomy 30:19)

Beloved, please accept Jesus and choose heaven. It is for your own sake, your own good. Once your life is over, it will be too late.

.

CHAPTER 31
MY COUSIN RONNIE

My lovely cousin Ronnie was a very kind and caring soul. He was quiet and shy with a winning smile, was a great chef, and was very versatile. When Peter and I were ministering in Trinidad, he took the time to drive us to the south of the island. When he wasn't able to drive us himself, he arranged for a friend to do so. He wanted to make sure that we were safe. We shared about Jesus with Ronnie a few times.

A few years ago, I received a telephone call that my cousin, who was not even forty years of age, had died from a heart attack. Everyone was shocked, as Ronnie was a robust young man. This was such a sudden blow. My greatest concern was for his salvation. Did Ronnie make things right with God? Was he ready to meet the Lord Jesus Christ?

Ronnie's funeral was held at the Caroni River, where Hindus are cremated. I was in Moravian Falls, North Carolina, and was in tears and great grief. As I was kneeling in prayer, in anguish of soul, it weighed heavily on my heart to have some sort of assurance about my cousin's salvation.

"Lord, if it is Your will, would you allow me to know about Ronnie?"

Suddenly, the Lord opened up my spiritual eyes and gave me a vision. My dear cousin Ronnie was shyly standing in the middle of a group of young ladies who had their arms entwined. They were gracefully circling around him in a kind of holy dance. He was smiling as they welcomed him into heaven! What peace flooded my soul when I saw this.

But then I thought, Why did no one tell me about Ronnie's salvation?

That evening, I spoke with my Uncle Sone on the telephone. What a report he had! For one whole month before passing away, Ronnie had visited him every day, asking many questions about Jesus and heaven. Sone said, "Prem, I didn't spare him! I told him everything he needed to know about heaven and hell. I told him that heaven is where Jesus is, but hell is where every unbeliever goes, and that is where they will stay for all eternity, with the devil. I also told him that there are no unbelievers in hell, but they all believed too late."

I was overjoyed! I told my uncle that if I were right there with him, I would give him a hug for speaking the truth with love and concern, and not sugar-coating the precious Gospel for fear of family or anyone. Ronnie heard the Gospel again and again for a whole month.

Also, his mother, my dear Aunt Lawatee, shared with me that, for several days before his passing, she heard him playing the same song over and over in his room. She was able to listen to the words. It was a Christian song, "Across the Bridge, There's No More Sorrow" by Jim Reeves. How Ronnie got that song, no one knows. My aunt said she knocked on his door and asked him why he was playing that song over and over again. He said, "I'm okay, Mom. Don't worry. Don't worry."

My cousin Ronnie went to be with the Lord. I understood why the Lord gave me a vision of Ronnie in heaven. He comforted my heart by answering my prayer, and then confirmed the vision through Uncle Sone and Aunt Lawatee.

You know, sometimes we don't share the Gospel because we are afraid of what people might think, or that our boldness might hurt their feelings, or some such thing. God wants us to be bold witnesses for Jesus because He wants all people to be saved. As it says in 2 Peter 3:9:

The Lord is not slack concerning His promise, as some men count slackness; but is longsuffering to us-ward, not willing that any should perish, but that all should come to repentance.

And while we must be bold and without compromise, we must also share the Gospel with love and compassion. Balance is a key word in sharing the Gospel with anyone.

"Please, Lord, If You Don't Mind..."

I am now in my sixties, and became a Christian over thirty years ago. Naturally, the older members of my family would be expected to pass away as time went on. However, one day I asked the Lord to help me understand why, after saving some of my loved ones, He took them away from this earth. His answer was very comforting.

The Lord said to me that for some, it was their time to go home. However, others were taken away because they were not strong enough to withstand the attacks of the devil, and eventually they would have fallen back into their old religious ways of life, thereby losing their souls.

Well, that is a good God! As it says in Job 1:21–22:

The LORD gave, and the LORD hath taken away; blessed be the Name of the LORD.

In all this Job sinned not, nor charged God foolishly.

As a Hindu, I had been to funerals where I saw the terrible hopelessness, and heard the awful screams, of those who

177

grieved for their loved ones, even in my own family. Along with all my relatives, I, too, screamed and wailed greatly, because we had no hope for the deceased. We knew only emptiness, hopelessness, and grief.

However, in Christianity we have the love, hope, and promises of the living and true God. We have the blessed hope of the resurrection!

As it says in 1 Peter 1:3–4:

Blessed be the God and Father of our Lord Jesus Christ, Which according to His abundant mercy hath begotten us again unto a lively hope by the resurrection of Jesus Christ from the dead,

To an inheritance incorruptible, and undefiled, and that fadeth not away, reserved in heaven for you.

We hurt so much when they are gone. We grieve, we remember their love and kindness, we feel so lonely without them. Precious one, we have hope! Through it all, healing starts to take effect as we remember that there is hope in Jesus Christ. All true believers in Jesus Christ will meet again one great day.

Meanwhile, dearly beloved, they are in heaven with our Creator and Redeemer. They are safe, well, whole, and happier than anyone on this dark earth. They are forever in the Lord's holy presence! May the wonderful promises we have been given in the Bible strengthen us to live each day with true purpose, knowing that one day we will see our loved ones again. What a blessed hope!

CHAPTER 32
TWO DREAMS COME TRUE

Over ten years ago, Peter and I spent some time with a couple who had been in Christian ministry for over twenty-five years, but had never been recognized by the church as full-fledged ministers of the Gospel.

Within a month of meeting them, the Lord gave me a dream. In it, the wife was asking her husband, "Who is going to ordain us?" Feeling impressed by the Holy Spirit that we were to ordain them, I answered, "The Lord said we have to ordain you." When I shared the dream with them, they were excited and told us that they had been praying about this for a long time, but no doors had opened.

Before the day of their ordination, while we were praying over them, the spirit of prophecy came over me. I said – almost sang – the words, "Come and get it while it's hot!" Then I saw a huge pot of chili. When I told them what the Lord had shown me, the brother confirmed what I saw by saying that he had the same vision the week before while driving, but had not shared it with his wife yet. The Lord also revealed that they would be moving to British Columbia.

Pastors Peter and Deborah Berlenbach now live in Abbotsford, British Columbia, and are the founders and senior pastors of Face to Face Ministries. Part of their ministry plan is to feed the homeless. "Come and get it while it's hot!"

As they are faithful servants of the Lord, He is much glorified in their lives and ministry. They experience the supernatural in a remarkable way, and the glory cloud of the Lord has been seen in their services.

Behold, I will do a new thing; now it shall spring forth; shall ye not know it? I will even make a way in the wilderness, and rivers in the desert. (Isaiah 43:19)

And they were all amazed, and they glorified God, and were filled with fear, saying, We have seen strange things today. (Luke 5:26)

Thou art the God that doest wonders: Thou hast declared Thy strength among the people. (Psalm 77:14)

And they went forth, and preached every where, the Lord working with them, and confirming the Word with signs following. Amen. (Mark 16:20)

God is doing a new thing in these last days, but some will miss out on the blessings because they simply can't believe that these supernatural signs and wonders are from God.

Another Dream Comes True

Although Louise was away from church for a year and a half, we still met and had coffee together. I never asked about her plans to return to church, as she was in her late sixties and was old enough to decide. My role was to support her.

In a dream very early one Sunday morning, I heard the voice of the Lord saying, "Louise, it is time to come back to church."

Before church that morning, I telephoned Louise and shared my dream. She replied, "Pastor, this has to be the Lord. Last night at about nine o'clock, I was walking in my kitchen and saying to the Lord, 'Lord, it's time for me to go back to church.'" Louise came to the service that morning, bringing a year and a half of tithes.

Sister Louise has been a faithful supporter of the ministry for many years now. Whenever I have a dream about her, she holds her breath, wondering what's coming. It's so funny to see!

CHAPTER 33
LEARNING TO FORGIVE

Because of the pain and rejection that I had experienced in the past, I was unstable in my emotions. This caused me to make foolish decisions, which in turn added to my already confused state. So, one of the first things I had to learn when I gave my heart to the Lord Jesus Christ was how to forgive.

First, I had to allow my Father to examine my own heart and do some major spiritual surgery on me before I was able to forgive others. I had to acknowledge and confess the many failures of my past. I had to take responsibility for things I did, things I didn't do which I should have done, and things I intended to do which would have caused pain to others.

I have my flaws, believe me. I continue to learn and grow, and sometimes it can be very painful. This is a fact of life for all of us, whether we like it or not. Along the way, I have had to walk in some very difficult places, but the faithful God of heaven continues to carry me when the journey seems too difficult or too long. God's grace is always sufficient as we trust Him to take us through.

I had to learn to forgive my family who didn't understand. After my conversion, having to walk alone without my family's love and support was an extremely painful place for me to be. Many a night, I cried myself to sleep. I had to cry out to God for His help and strength when I was termed an outcast, a traitor to my race, a curse, and other unpleasant names. Yet, the Lord proved Himself faithful to His Word, and it is a miracle to see what God has already done.

One of my biggest tests in forgiving came one day in an airport in Canada. God arranged for me to cross paths with the first man I married, who had abused me so terribly in every way. Here I was, a survivor of domestic violence in its worst forms, facing the very person who had so badly damaged and nearly destroyed me.

Because I was growing in my faith by the grace of God, I felt no fear when I saw him. However, I must admit that the temptation came to me in a whisper, "Now is the time to let him have it! Take your pocketbook and give him one, square on his head! Then smack him real hard and run off!" In one moment, I could see myself acting like Olive in the Popeye cartoon, and I was glad that I hadn't eaten spinach that morning. However, knowing that I had a choice to make, I found myself silently praying, "Lord, help me! Please, Lord, I really need Your help!"

Thank God for His love and grace! The Lord had me politely greet him, give him a Christian tract on salvation, and tell him that I had forgiven him and was praying for him. God put compassion in my heart for this lost soul. He seemed stunned, and nodded his head as he quietly acknowledged my words. I continue to pray for salvation for this family.

I have learned that forgiving someone doesn't necessarily mean remaining in the same environment. Depending on your situation, make sure that you are safe. Always seek help. It is very important that we forgive those who have wounded us, whether it is a spouse, friend, neighbor, pastor, in-law, or whoever.

Carrying a grudge creates bitterness, which is a poison of the soul, and which acts as a poison in the human body. It affects every area of our lives, hindering both our mind and our walk with the Lord. We must forgive those who have hurt us, pray for them, and allow God to heal us. He is a God of justice, grace, and mercy. As we obey Him in all things, He is quite capable of handling every situation. He vindicates in due time.

Being in the ministry for over three decades, I have experienced all kinds of pain and heartbreak, which are never pleasant nor easy. However, as King David did, we need to encourage ourselves and one another in the Lord. The wise use their speech to heal – not to discourage and destroy. We need to know when to speak and when to remain silent.

I have been so wounded by others that it took me a long time to recover. In one incident, I felt as if my heart was splitting in two. My spirit was crushed. The worst part of it was that I did nothing to cause it. Frustration was directed at me, and I was humiliated in the presence of others. Even after I forgave this person, I still hurt badly. Sometimes, pain doesn't just go away. It is not good to say to someone who is hurting, "Get over it." I needed to be healed. I was even told that I was being childish. When healing is needed, that is not being childish. Healing is a process. We need to extend compassion with understanding.

Can we hear the cry of a soul? If not, then we have lost our way.

However, God is a good God, and He heard my cry. He dried my tears and healed my hurt. After a while, the Lord told me to go to the person and show His love. I did, but not without hesitation. My painful experience had put some fear in my heart. I shared it with Peter and asked him to pray with me. Thank God, I was able to overcome and go back to that particular church. When the person saw me, he came over, hugged me, and cried. I was glad to have obeyed the Lord as I saw the hand of God at work through this unfortunate experience.

Let's stay focused on the Lord as we pray for those who wound us. The Lord will vindicate the upright in heart. He knows how to take care of it. I have seen the victorious hand of the Lord turn many things around for His glory. So, if you have been wounded through no fault of your own, wait upon the Lord, and He will fix the matter in His own loving way. Amen. If you are at fault, sincerely confess your wrongdoing to the Lord, and ask for His forgiveness and cleansing. Thank Him for His goodness. Then do what is necessary to make things right. He wants you to acknowledge your sin so that He can extend His mercy to you and start the healing process.

CHAPTER 34
HEALING TESTIMONIES

Who His own self [Jesus] *bare our sins in His own body on the tree, that we, being dead to sins, should live unto righteousness: by Whose stripes ye were healed.* (1 Peter 2:24)

Bless the LORD, O my soul: and all that is within me, bless His holy Name.

Bless the LORD, O my soul, and forget not all His benefits:

Who forgiveth all thine iniquities; Who healeth all thy diseases. (Psalm 103:1–3)

Oh that men would praise the LORD for His goodness, and for His wonderful works to the children of men! (Psalm 107:21)

Insomuch that the multitude wondered, when they saw the dumb to speak, the maimed to be whole, the lame to walk, and the blind to see: and they glorified the God of Israel. (Matthew 15:31)

A Miracle Baby

Preet, whom I met while working at the bank and who is still my very dear friend, was devastated after her doctor told her that she could not conceive. She and her husband, Ron, had been trying to have a child for over three years. In my first year of being a Christian, the Holy Spirit impressed upon my heart to prophesy that He was going to bless her with a child that year.

Six weeks later, Preet conceived. However, during a routine checkup, the doctor informed her that he could not detect signs of life in the unborn child. Devastated once again, Preet and I stood on the word which the Lord had spoken, and prayed together in child-like faith.

Much to the joy of her parents, a healthy, beautiful baby girl, Rachel Grace, was born to them that year, and has grown up to be a fine young lady. The Lord God gave them the desire of their hearts, and His word was fulfilled. May He always be glorified!

A Medical Miracle

While I was praying over the telephone for Sister Dilu from Sri Lanka, the word of the Lord came in prophecy that He wanted to bless her with a child. "That's impossible," she told me. They already had two daughters, and she had taken medical measures to not have any more children.

Two months later, the doctor was stunned as he confirmed that she was with child. "How could you be pregnant?" he queried. "I myself performed the operation!"

However, my Father had spoken, and He did it. His word will never return void. This time, the Lord blessed the family with a son, Josiah, whom Peter and I met when the family visited Canada. May the Lord Jesus Christ be glorified!

Ear Surgery Canceled

Shewaye had a very painful, punctured eardrum and was booked for surgery. After she was anointed with oil and prayed over, the pain left. A further check by her doctor revealed that her eardrum had been healed. The surgery was canceled. To God be all the glory!

Finger Surgery Canceled

A few years later, Shewaye had a growth, as big as a dime, under the skin of one of her fingers. She was scheduled for surgery, but canceled it when the Lord spoke to her heart to receive prayer instead.

As I held her hand in mine and prayed, the growth melted right under my finger. To God be all the glory, now and forever! One Healer – Jesus Christ, the Great Physician.

Growth Falls off Palm

A child's palm was diseased with a bloody outgrowth. Every three weeks, the doctors burnt off the growth, but it kept returning.

One morning after the child, Amanda, was prayed over, the growth fell off her palm. The fire of the Holy Ghost burnt it off once and for all. Glory to our Lord Jesus!

Nose Surgery Canceled

Another child had a growing flesh in his nose, and was booked for surgery. After he received prayer, the Lord healed him, and the surgery was canceled. To God be all the glory!

Snatched from Death

A few coma patients have been healed. Here are two reports:

I was asked to go and pray for Sean, a young man who was in a coma. His mother told me that the doctors had given him only a few more hours to live. After he received prayer in the intensive care unit, the machines started to "jingle."

The nurses came running, thinking that this young man was dying. Rather, our merciful Lord Jesus Christ met with him, and he was totally healed. To God be all the glory!

The Lord Heals Another Coma Patient

Michelle, a sister in Christ, was visiting Canada from Trinidad. She suddenly became seriously ill and was rushed to the hospital, where she fell into a coma. Thirteen days later, her family came to a Sunday service at the church, telling us about her condition.

That evening, I accompanied them to the hospital to pray for their sister. In the intensive care unit, the nurse asked me to put on a hospital gown, gloves, and mask as the doctors "did not know what they were dealing with." When I told the nurse that I wanted to remove my gloves to lay hands on the patient and pray, she warned me that I would be doing so at my own risk.

After anointing Michelle with oil, I laid my hands on her and prayed.

To the glory of God, on Monday, the respirator was removed. By Wednesday, Michelle was going to the bathroom unaided. On Saturday, when I telephoned to see how she was doing, her brother asked me to hold the line. "She is coming through the door," he said. She had been discharged from the hospital.

Eight days later, our dear sister Michelle braved the snow, ice, and cold to come to church to share her testimony.

Isn't our Lord Jesus wonderful? He is, and always will be, the greatest Healer! Bless His most holy Name!

Healed of Cancer

A Christian couple telephoned us for prayer because the wife had cancer. As Peter and I prayed for her, she was overcome and fell in the Spirit. Her husband continued to pray with us for her healing. A few days later, when the doctors operated on her, they were amazed to find no cancer.

Jesus does all things well. Praise Him!

Deliverance from Evil Spirits

Through a referral, a Christian brother brought his wife to the church because she was possessed by evil spirits. He was a believer, but had married outside the Christian faith. While I was praying for her, the Holy Spirit revealed what spirits were to be cast out. As I obeyed the Lord's instructions, the lady was immediately delivered, and confessed Jesus Christ as Lord!

Because of this tremendous testimony, the rest of her family became Christians. May God the Father, God the Son, and God the Holy Ghost be glorified! Praise the Lord!

Another Case of Deliverance

Di, a church member, needed deliverance from evil spirits. As I prayed for her, she fell on the floor as if unconscious. An evil spirit spoke through her, giving someone's name. It told me to open the window as it wanted to leave the building that way. I stood my ground and commanded, "In Jesus' Name, you take orders from me. I don't take orders from you. You leave right now!" It was cast out, and Di was totally set free. Praise the living and true God forever!

When I asked if she recognized the name that the spirit had mentioned, Di shared that a close family member by that name had been heavily involved in the occult before she died.

New Hair Growth

One Sunday morning, a brother from Brazil visited the church with his family. He found us through the internet, and needed prayer. He had a rare condition which caused all his hair to fall out, and which his doctor in Brazil said was incurable. Even his eyebrows were affected.

A year later when he returned to visit us, he was elated, and we could see why. Our Lord Jesus had touched our brother and reversed the words of the doctor. Hair had grown on both the top of his head and his eyebrows!

For with God nothing shall be impossible. (Luke 1:37)

Our brother also told us that he sent a picture of his new hair to the doctor in Brazil through his sister-in-law. The doctor was stunned to see the results. She, in turn, was able to witness to him about the love and power of our Lord Jesus Christ. To God be all the glory!

Healed of a Kidney Stone

Another time, this same brother visited us to receive prayer for a kidney stone. He was scheduled for surgery the following week. On the day of his surgery, he had already changed into the hospital gown and was in the waiting room when another doctor came in and told him that his surgery was canceled. The surgeon who was scheduled to do the operation was unavailable. Our brother said that he saw the hand of the Lord in the change of plan, and thought that He must have something else in mind.

He went home and passed the kidney stone – without pain! I was told that, medically, one of the most excruciating things a man can experience is to pass a kidney stone.

Our wonderful Lord Jesus operated on him and healed him completely. May He always be glorified!

The Master of the Waves

Do you know the Master,
The Only One Who saves?
His Name is JESUS,
And He is the Master of the waves.

He calms the storms of life,
He gives peace where there is strife.
He is the Lord of Glory and Grace,
So, get set to run this Eternal Race.

Is your heart troubled sometimes?
Is there a void which aches to be filled?
Give it willingly to the Master,
And He shall mold you as He wills.

He is faithful – He never fails,
Don't be in doubt – just reach out in faith.
Read the Bible and get to know Him,
And your spiritual eyes will never grow dim.

For this Master of the waves
Is within a breath's take.
Call upon His Holy Name,
And you shall never be the same.

Yield to the Lord Jesus above,
With all your heart and soul;
And someday you will enjoy life,
In a Land where you will never grow old.

For the Master of the waves is there,
To direct you as you cross the Sea.
He holds in His Hand, Life and Death.
So, get set, for Only He has the Eternal Key.

—Prema Pelletier

CHAPTER 35
HOW TO RECEIVE SALVATION

I would like to share with you the most important truth that I have learned in my life's journey: Whether we realize it or not, we all need Jesus.

The Bible says in John 3:16–17:

For God so loved the world, that He gave His only begotten Son, that whosoever believeth in Him should not perish, but have everlasting life.

For God sent not His Son into the world to condemn the world; but that the world through Him might be saved.

The Bible tells us that we have all sinned, even good, moral people. Through the sin of Adam, the first man created by God, the whole world is born into sin. I thought that I was a good person. Yet, I was a sinner, just as we all are sinners, whether we acknowledge it or not.

As it is written, There is none righteous, no, not one. (Romans 3:10)

For all have sinned, and come short of the glory of God. (Romans 3:23)

Furthermore, the Bible tells us that there is a penalty for sin, which is eternal judgment.

For the wages of sin is death. (Romans 6:23)

However, the good news is that God does not want us to perish in our sins and be lost in hell for all eternity. Rather, He wants us to repent of our sins, which involves turning from our sinful ways.

The Lord is not slack concerning His promise, as some men count slackness; but is longsuffering to us-ward, not willing that any should perish, but that all should come to repentance. (2 Peter 3:9)

However, what about the sins that we have already committed? And what about sins which we commit even after we repent and strive to live a holy life? What can ever save us from the penalty of having committed those sins?

That is why the Lord Jesus Christ came to this earth and died on the Cross.

For the wages of sin is death; but the gift of God is eternal life through Jesus Christ our Lord. (Romans 6:23)

Neither is there salvation in any other: for there is none other Name [none other than Jesus Christ] *under heaven given among men, whereby we must be saved.* (Acts 4:12)

The Bible tells us that Jesus is the only person Who has ever, and will ever, live a sinless life. When He died on the Cross of Calvary, He did not die for sins which He had committed. Rather, the Bible explains that His death was the only sacrifice that God will accept for the forgiveness of *our* sins.

In His love and mercy, God provided a way whereby we can be forgiven of our sins and can spend eternity in His glorious presence. When we repent, the precious Blood of Jesus that He shed on the Cross washes away our sins and wipes our slate clean.

196

In the terrible agony that Christ suffered for us on Calvary, God did His part in providing for our eternal salvation. Out of His grace and goodness, He offers us forgiveness and salvation through the shed Blood of His Son.

However, the Bible tells us that it is up to us to do our part, and that is to receive His gracious offer.

Come now, and let us reason together, saith the LORD: though your sins be as scarlet, they shall be as white as snow; though they be red like crimson, they shall be as wool. (Isaiah 1:18)

In faith, we must accept the Lord Jesus Christ as our personal Lord and Savior, which means that we receive Him as the ruler of our lives. We surrender to His Lordship.

When the Lord Jesus was crucified, He died, and then was buried in a garden tomb hewn out of rock. But, to the glory of God, on the third day Jesus was raised up from the dead by the power of the Holy Spirit!

Christians worship a living God, not a dead one. The Bible tells us that death could not hold Jesus in the grave. He is the conqueror of death, hell, and the grave!

Wherefore God also hath highly exalted Him, and given Him a Name which is above every name:

That at the Name of Jesus every knee should bow, of things in heaven, and things in earth, and things under the earth;

And that every tongue should confess that Jesus Christ is Lord, to the glory of God the Father. (Philippians 2:9–11)

Without God's forgiveness, you are lost forever. Please do not wait another moment to experience this great privilege and blessing which God so freely offers you. At one time, I was a lost, lonely, depressed, suicidal basket case, fit for an asylum. Today, look what the LORD has done! He can change your life too. He wants to. He will give you hope and joy and peace. As you pray for God's forgiveness and sincerely seek Him, He will make Himself real to you. He is real. He is alive!

Think about the fact that God says that you are a sinner. Now allow the Holy Spirit to convict your heart of your sins. Allow Him to draw you to your Heavenly Father through His Son Jesus Christ by sincerely praying the following prayer. As you do, Jesus Christ will come into your heart. He will help you to live for Him daily.

"Dear God in heaven, I come to you as a lost sinner. Thank You for sending Your only begotten Son, Jesus Christ, to die for my sins. I repent of my sins, and I ask for Your forgiveness through the precious shed Blood of the Lord Jesus Christ. Please wash away all my sins through the Blood of Your Son Jesus. In faith, I now receive Jesus as my Lord and Savior. Thank You, Jesus, for coming into my heart through Your Holy Spirit. Thank You, Father, for Your great grace and mercy upon me. In Jesus' Name I pray, AMEN!"

Your next step is to get a Bible. You may want to start reading the Gospels – Matthew, Mark, Luke and John – to learn about the Lord Jesus. Please get into a good Bible-believing church to help you grow in your newfound faith.

God bless you as you begin your journey in the right direction with our Lord Jesus Christ. May the Holy Spirit always lead you.

By God's Grace, see you in heaven!

Glory be to the Father, the Son, and the Holy Spirit. Amen.

Prema, a convert from Hinduism, was called to full-time Christian service in 1988. In 1995, she was ordained to the Gospel Ministry by the Jacksonville Theological Seminary, Jacksonville, Florida. Prema is a Revivalist who preaches the Word of God with Holy Ghost fire. She and her husband, Peter, planted and pastored Rivers of Living Water Church in Toronto, Canada, for twenty years. Peter is an anointed Bible teacher and gifted administrator. They now reside in North Carolina, USA.

Contact Information:
Prema Pelletier
PO Box 875
Moravian Falls, NC 28654-0875
USA
Email: *PremaPelletier77@gmail.com*